Vocabulary NOW!

44 strategies all teachers can use

Valerie Auer & Marguerite Hartill

Published by Seidlitz Education
San Antonio, TX
wwwseidlitzeducation.com

To obtain permission to use material from this work, please submit a
written request to Seidlitz Education Permissions Department,
56 Via Regalo, San Clemente, CA 92673

For related titles and support materials visit www.seidlitzeducation.com.

4.14

acknowledgments

First and foremost, it is important to express our thanks to all the administrators and teachers in Texas and beyond who provided numerous opportunities to work with them and learn from them. A special thank you goes to the many skilled educators in the Fredericksburg ISD and Irving ISD. We are especially grateful for the support and learning opportunities provided by Mich Robertson. Her willingness to try new vocabulary activities and provide evidence of the final product was proof positive that students were developing academic language.

We owe a great deal of gratitude to the staff at Seidlitz Education. John Seidlitz worked tirelessly to make sure this book was both teacher and student friendly. We would also like to thank Kathy Belanger, Nancy Motley, Mónica Lara, Stefanie Brown, Alma Seidlitz, and Michelle Belanger for their constant support and feedback. A special thanks goes to Annie Griffin-Boerm who offered comments and advice on the many different methods for developing vocabulary for students. As always, we thank Anne-Charlotte Patterson for her creative expertise and talent as we designed this book.

Valerie is completely indebted to her parents, John and Carol Auer, and friend, Kris Barnes, for helping her babysit/nanny her precious son, Zane Auer. With their care and Zane's love, patience, and willingness to endure time apart from Mommy, this resource book was created. Now, many teachers throughout the state of Texas and beyond will be able to give their students the gift of academic language.

Marguerite would like to thank her husband, Richard, and her daughters, Christina and Lisa, for their constant support and feedback during this project. They are always an endless source of encouragement and praise. Then, there's Buddy, her little dachshund, who "industriously" sits by her side as she writes; he provides infinite inspiration to sit and carry on. And, of course, a big thank you goes to John Seidlitz. He is a pathfinder in the field of education. We could not do without his vision and knowledge.

With the involvement and participation of all the people who, directly and indirectly, helped in the compilation of this book, we know we have worked together to give students across our nation the gift of academic language.

table of contents

introduction

that teachers and students struggle with academic language…in different ways of course. First, let's talk about students. Every year, students are expected to understand hundreds of new vocabulary words in science, math, social studies, and English language arts. Then, they are expected to use those words fluently as they solve problems, engage in experiments, read about historical/political events, and interpret literature in their classrooms. Since students need guidance from teachers, a teacher's role is very important. While teachers have the responsibility for teaching content, they have to be sure their students understand classroom and textbook language. With creativity and repetition, this task can be completed with great assurance.

This book does not "speak" in the theoretical language seen in vocabulary acquisition studies, but it does use the work of many vocabulary/linguistic/educational theorists for its foundation. Such giants as Robert Marzano (2004), Michael Graves (2006), Isabel Beck (2002), Margaret McKeown (2002), and Linda Kucan (2002) have established the groundwork, and *Vocabulary NOW!* puts their research to work in activities to stimulate word recognition, ideas, problem solving, writing, and metacognition. The best part about this book is that while it is a teacher resource, the activities are for students. *Vocabulary NOW!* lets teachers and students take out their vocabulary tools and start to learn. Build a better future. Construct a new beginning. Design a successful career.

While the activities in this book are meant to give students many opportunities to work with the words they are learning in class, one of the best ways teachers can help students develop vocabulary is to encourage them to become readers. Whether students are interested in fiction or non-fiction, math or science, history or literature, there is something for all students to read. When students read, they become comfortable with words, and ultimately that is the goal for all teachers. Students who read, read, and read even more, exhibit comprehension levels that increase exponentially. As teachers encourage students to read outside the classroom, they leave a powerful legacy.

Oftentimes, math and science teachers will have to step outside the box to engage their students in some of the vocabulary activities in this book, but the effort is worth the outcome. Use the activities in this book to give students a firm foundation in the building blocks of language — the academic terminology — they need to read and respond to the math problems they examine in textbooks, the science experiments they perform in class, the social studies events they study in history, and the literature they read and interpret in English language arts.

critical background information

When is language born?

Learning new vocabulary begins when a child is a tiny baby and continues for a lifetime, and the words children learn and use indicate how well and how much they will achieve. The task for educators then is to find the best ways to teach vocabulary.

Think about the time you first learned to tie your shoes. The bow probably didn't turn out flawlessly the first time, and the second or third time didn't look picture-perfect either. But, by the time you tied that bow seventeen times, you really tied the perfect bow! And so it is with children learning language. The more they use a word in spoken language and in writing, the more they become comfortable with the word. Once the word finds its way into permanent memory — a repository of background knowledge — it becomes part of their repertoire, and they use it without thinking too much about it. It's just like tying shoes! We don't think about it when we are in the process, it just happens.

The beauty of learning language is the ability to begin a conversation, speak fluently, and engage confidently and creatively…whether it be in writing or in person. The National Institute for Literacy (2006) has also highlighted the importance, noting that, "Once vocabulary words have been selected, teachers should consider how to make repeated exposures to the word or concept productive and enjoyable."

With those words in mind, there are two indispensable ideas for learning new vocabulary.

First, it is essential to build background knowledge; second it is necessary to create opportunities for multiple exposures to new words. When students practice these steps, they begin to own the new words.

Why is vocabulary development so essential?

The German author, Goethe, once said, "The limits of my language are the limits of my universe." How very true this is when we think about our students and their ability to express themselves orally and in writing. The expression of ideas, thoughts, and experiences could be limitless if students have the necessary vocabulary to communicate. After all, vocabulary is the way a student shows who they are. For instance, a student in science class can say, in very rudimentary English, "How does a boat float?" But, with better vocabulary skills, he could say, "There is a photograph in our textbook of an enormous ship floating on the water. It is so big, it seems it would sink. Can you explain the technology to me?" The level of sophistication in the second example is evident, and the impression it makes on the listener is predictable. When comparing the two sentences, it certainly appears as if the speaker of the second sentence is clearly more knowledgeable and articulate.

Communication skills mean the difference between success and failure, especially for at-risk students on the secondary level (RAND Reading Study Group, 2002; NICHD Report of the National Reading Panel, 2000). The reason for this is simple. Vocabulary at the middle and high school level becomes increasingly more difficult because students need to learn the academic vocabulary of science, math, social studies, and language arts. Academic vocabulary is the language found in textbooks, and it is the language of assessment. With the introduction of new vocabulary, native English speakers, as well as English Language Learners (ELLs), can find the language they encounter in class very confusing. When students struggle to understand the academic vocabulary in each subject area, they fall farther and farther behind in their studies. According to O'Neal and Ringler (2010), "academic English is virtually a new language that must be taught to all students in order for them to be successful." In fact, "....all learners, regardless of proficiency in their dialect or standard English, must be proficient in academic English to be successful in academic settings."

To expose students to academic vocabulary on a regular basis can and should be part of every classroom because the complexity of the language grows as students transition between grade levels.

Which vocabulary words do students need to know?

"The difference between the almost right word and the right word is really a large matter – it's the difference between the lightning bug and the lightning." – Mark Twain

Selecting the right vocabulary words to teach students can be difficult too. When deciding which words to teach, some words (like *omit*) need only a brief mention with a quick definition to ensure student comprehension. Just a synonym (like *leave out* or *delete*) provides a quick and easy explanation for the word *omit*, and it is one that students grasp quickly. On the other hand, most vocabulary words need to be taught on a much deeper level, and they need to be reinforced multiple times during the course of study.

When choosing which vocabulary words to teach on a deeper level, the rule of thumb is to choose 4-6 words per week for the content being studied. Instead of choosing vocabulary words from high-

frequency lists, Marzano and Pickering (2005) say that, "Comprehension will increase by 33% when vocabulary instruction focuses on specific words important to the content."

When vocabulary is selected, it is important to refer to state standards to be sure that vocabulary lessons keep students on track for learning. Keeping these ideas in mind, it is crucial to remember that students will not understand content unless they understand the vocabulary.

Marzano and Pickering (2005) believe that a person's knowledge of any topic can be summarized in the terms relevant to a topic. Best practices show that vocabulary should never be taught in isolation. For better understanding, vocabulary words should always be taught in context.

In addition to making decisions about the 4-6 vocabulary terms to use every week, teachers can employ the guidelines set in Tiers I, II, and III for vocabulary acquisition (Beck, McKeown, & Kucan, 2002).

- Tier I words are common terms (often referred to as high-frequency words) that students hear in everyday classroom discourse. These are

words that are familiar to most students. The exception will be with some English Language Learners.

- Tier II words are terms that are best suited for explicit instruction by both content area and literacy specialists because they appear in a variety of texts and can be found across the curriculum.

- Tier III words are specific to a particular subject area, appear infrequently, and are taught by content area teachers.

Where do students learn new vocabulary?

The answer to that question is ….everywhere. Students hear new words when they go to the movies, watch television, converse with friends, read a book, or examine the instructions for a new electronic device.

However, some of the most important vocabulary connections are made when students read for pleasure. Research supports the fact that encouraging personal student reading is the single most powerful thing teachers can do to increase vocabulary (Anderson & Nagy, 1992; Stahl & Fairbanks, 1986).

While academic vocabulary is learned in the classroom, personal reading selections are vitally important to a student's background knowledge. Silent Sustained Reading (SSR) programs have a proven track record of enhancing students' knowledge and skills, especially for those who do not read outside of school (Marzano, 2004).

When a student reads, there are multiple opportunities to see how words are used in our language. The only caveat is that the SSR program needs to be continuous over many years because it is a cumulative process.

What is the best way for students to learn vocabulary?

All avenues to learn vocabulary are important. As Marzano (2004) states, there is a six-step process for direct vocabulary instruction.

The six-step process includes the following:

1. The teacher describes the vocabulary terms.
2. The students construct their own descriptions of the terms.
3. The students construct nonlinguistic representations.
4. The teacher provides opportunities for students to review and add to their knowledge of the terms.
5. The students use the terms interactively in class.
6. The students apply vocabulary terms in word games.

Using the six-steps method combined with Silent Sustained Reading (SSR) is a powerful way to enhance academic background knowledge.

How do students learn vocabulary?

"Any idea, plan, or purpose may be placed in the mind through repetition of thought."
- Napoleon Hill

Students learn vocabulary words through the interaction of two factors: (1) the ability to process and store information, and (2) the number and frequency of academically oriented experiences (Marzano, 2004).

Repetition, or multiple exposures to words, is paramount for students learning new vocabulary. The more attempts students make to use a word, the more the brain enforces the motion. Word tasks offered to students at least three times per week over a period of months shows students the way to use language, and then words become part of the permanent memory. Cognitive psychologists refer to this innate ability as fluid intelligence. Cattell (1987) defined fluid intelligence as the ability to process information and store it in permanent memory. Once a word is part of permanent memory, the word has been learned, and it can be retrieved at any time. It's just like tying your shoes!

vocabulary beginnings

1. Scanning
2. Visual Word Wall

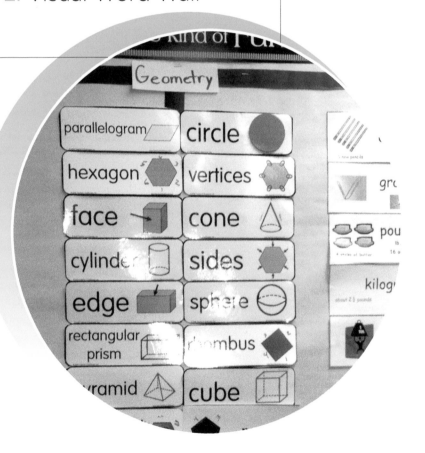

1 Scanning

What it's all about

Scanning is a strategy used to help teachers determine the essential vocabulary that students may not understand in an academic text, and it is done prior to reading. With a list of new vocabulary, the words can be pre-taught. By pre-teaching new vocabulary, student comprehension of the text to be read and studied will increase. Stahl and Fairbanks (1986) demonstrate that student comprehension will expand 33% when specific key terms are pre-taught to students before reading. Conducting a scan of an academic text is the perfect way to start. It dramatically increases student comprehension and lowers the emotional barriers (affective filter) when encountering challenging text.

Directions

1. Have students start at the bottom of the page and scan up to the top to survey the academic text for unfamiliar terms. Instruct students to underline or circle any words they are unable to define. By starting at the bottom of the page, the student can focus on individual words without trying to read the material. To encourage students to identify words, tell them to circle words they think others in class may not know either. This takes the pressure off "not knowing."

2. Have students generate a list of unfamiliar words or terms from the text and have them hand their lists to the teacher.

3. Make a master class list of the words the students have given, and distribute a copy to all students. *(Note: Avoid having more than ten words on the list. If more than ten words are needed for student comprehension, it is best to select another reading passage for this activity.)*

4. As a class, take the master list of words and create student-friendly definitions for each new vocabulary word. Many times, a simple synonym for the word is appropriate at this point. Make sure that the correct contextual definition for multiple meaning words is shared with students as well. For example, in social studies, the word *property* can mean ownership, but in science it means a specific quality or feature. *(Note: By sharing the task of defining new words, students have the chance to listen to the word as it is spoken and to hear the definitions their classmates offer.)*

EXTENSION ACTIVITIES

Have students complete the Four-Corners Word Model for selected words on p. 32.

Have students conduct a scan of released standardized test questions and answer choices to find unfamiliar academic terminology.

2 Visual Word Wall

What it's all about

Word Walls speak volumes... even as they stand silently in the classroom. On a Word Wall, students can see definitions, diagrams, drawings, designs of vocabulary words, high-frequency words, academic language, brick and mortar words, and word families. When creating a Word Wall, write the vocabulary words in bold print so students can see them easily from any part of the classroom. Word Walls can be placed in any content area classroom: social studies, science, math, English language arts, etc.

Posted in the classroom, words on the Word Wall stand ready to support students during reading and writing activities. Adding five words per week allows the wall to grow, and it encourages students to continue learning new words throughout the year.

Directions

1. Designate one area in the classroom for a Visual Word Wall.

2. Post single words, words with definitions, drawings of words, stories using words, or clippings from magazines or newspapers that contain the vocabulary words. Be sure that words are written large enough for students to see them from any place in the classroom.

3. Encourage students to look at the Word Wall for help during any written or oral activities conducted in class.

EXTENSION ACTIVITY

Send students searching for pictures that portray their vocabulary words in action, e.g., *chaos* could be found in the sports section, as one player tumbles onto others on the football field. Place the pictures students find on the Word Wall with the vocabulary word attached.

Math: Ask students to write a word problem using vocabulary Word Wall words.

Science: Ask students to write a description of a scientific procedure they have observed recently in class. Have students include three words from the Word Wall.

Social Studies: Ask students to describe a historical figure, historical event, or type of government they have studied recently in class. Have students include three words from the Word Wall in the description.

English Language Arts: Ask students to describe a character from a novel or short story they have read in class. Have students include three words from the Word Wall.

Provide a sentence starter for students using one vocabulary word. Ask students to continue the narrative using at least two other vocabulary words from the Word Wall.

Refer to words on the Word Wall while teaching.

word analysis

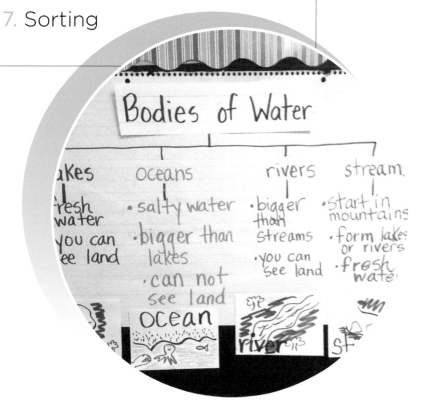

3 Analogies

What it's all about

Word analogies are word problems that challenge students to compare and contrast words in logical relationships. Analogies are most effective when students determine relationships of words they already know before creating analogies with new vocabulary words. By scaffolding prior knowledge with new knowledge, a strong foundation is set. Robert Marzano et al., (2001) includes creating analogies as an effective method of comparing and contrasting. It is one of nine high-yield strategies that increases comprehension by up to 45%.

Research shows that analogical thinking is a complex activity that requires students to engage in an in-depth analysis of content, and it requires them to determine similarities and differences (Alexander, 1984; Ratterman & Gentner, 1998).

To determine relationships in analogies, students have to find a link between the words. As they analyze word pairs, they have to decide what the first word pair establishes: synonyms, antonyms, cause and effect, part to whole, object to function, product to producer, geography, or measurement and time. *(Note: Words in both parts of an analogy mirror one another in parts of speech. For example, if there are two nouns on the left side of the analogy, there will be two nouns on the right side. If there is a noun and an adjective on one side, there will be a noun and adjective on the other side.)*

Given one word in the second part of the analogy, students have to select the correct word to complete the analogy. For example:

funny : hilarious :: hot : sizzling

Analogies often appear on standardized tests as word pairs. To ensure student success, it is important to model ways to create and complete analogies.

Directions

1. Show examples of analogies and discuss the types of relationships that exist, i.e., synonyms, antonyms, cause and effect, part to whole, object to function, product to producer, geography, or measurement and time.

2. Explain the structure of analogies. Tell students that the colon between the first two words is read "is to," and the double colon between the two pairs of words is read "as." For example: poverty : wealth :: sickness : health is read like this: poverty is to wealth as sickness is to health.

3. Establish that the relationship between the pairs is opposite, or antonyms.

4. Guide students in creating more analogies using the same relationships with words they already know.

5. Scaffold instruction by selecting two related words that students know and a third "new" word from the vocabulary list or Word Wall. Identify and discuss the relationship between the two known words.

6. Write the third word on the board followed by a colon and a blank. Ask students to generate possibilities for a word with the same relationship to the target word as the first two words have with each other.

7. Assign vocabulary words to students, or students can self-select words from the vocabulary list or Word Wall, and have them create their own analogies.

8. Discuss students' analogies as a group and place them on the Word Wall.

example

Vocabulary word: inaudible

Invisible : see :: inaudible : _____

Invisible : see :: inaudible : hear

EXTENSION ACTIVITY

Have students create 2-3 analogies that test the language power of a shoulder partner.

4 Word Nuances

What it's all about

A word or an idea can take on subtle differences in expression, meaning, or response when different age groups are considered. For example, a snowy day might mean great fun for a young child, a day off from school for a teenager, a longer commute for an adult, or an appointment postponed for an older person. If students use their vocabulary words to complete Word Nuances, they too will discover the way words have depth and complexity.

Directions

1. Select a word for students or have them choose a word they want to explore.

2. Ask students to explain what the word would mean to a young child, a teenager, an adult, and an older person. (See the example below.) Explain how a word can be interpreted, depending on the age group.

examples

English Language Arts: abashed

Young child: taking a cookie without asking only to find he/she has been discovered

Teenager: leaving today's assignment on the kitchen table

Adult: locking the keys in the car

Older person: being late for an appointment

Social Studies: tyranny

Young child: commands from an older sibling

Teenager: homework every night

Adult: demands of a 9-5 job

Older person: physical limitations

Math: sum

Young child: the total number of cookies he/she has

Teenager: the number of friends on Facebook

Adult: the number of vacation days at the end of the year

Older person: the number of grandchildren

Science: evaporates

Young child: puddles

Teenager: soda

Adult: coffee in a coffee pot

Older person: time with family (figuratively)

EXTENSION ACTIVITY

Have students write a conversation between two age groups, using two additional vocabulary words.

5 Concept Definition Map

What it's all about

Concept mapping helps students in two different ways. First, students can study a new word in depth. Second, concept mapping helps students define and describe unfamiliar words. To complete a concept map, students use a graphic organizer to identify the category/class, properties, or examples of the concept or target word.

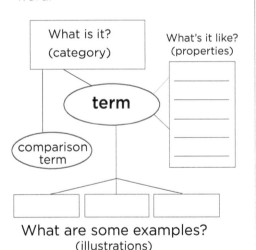

What is it? (category)

What's it like? (properties)

term

comparison term

What are some examples? (illustrations)

Directions

1. Distribute or have students draw a copy of the Concept Definition Map in the left column (Novak, Moon, Hoffman, & Canas, 2011).

2. Provide a target word or concept for students to insert in the center circle.

3. Have students work in groups of three to identify the category and properties on the concept map, i.e., What is it? What's it like?, etc.

4. Ask students to write some comparison terms in the left circle.

5. Have students work individually on three illustrations for the last question: What are some examples?

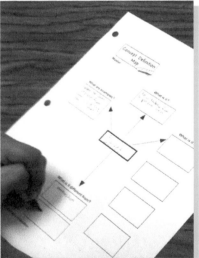

EXTENSION ACTIVITY

Have students focus on the column in the Concept Definition Map titled What's It Like? Ask students to list words that describe the term in the center circle.

6 Word Parts

What it's all about

A morpheme is a small part of a word that has meaning. Morphemes include affixes (prefixes and suffixes), base words, and Greek and Latin roots. Prefixes expand the meaning of a word while suffixes often change the part of speech when they are attached to a word. For example, the word antibiotic has three morphemes: anti-, bio, and -tic.

Learning about morphemes helps students build analytical skills, and it helps them deconstruct and understand unfamiliar words they encounter while reading. Morpheme instruction is most effective in context with known words.

Directions

1. Provide students with a list of morphemes which includes morphemes related to current classroom vocabulary. (A list of morphemes is included in the Appendix on page 78.)

2. Supply a list of simple definitions for the morphemes if the vocabulary words are new to students. If students have already had multiple exposures to the morphemes, do not include definitions. Instead, allow them to create the definitions.

3. Guide students as they work to divide the list into three parts: prefixes (morphemes at the beginning of a word), roots (morphemes that form the base of a word), and suffixes (morphemes that end a word).

4. Have students work in pairs to create words using the morphemes from the list. Allow them to create actual words or silly words.

5. Have pairs share one or two of their created words with the class.

6. Ask other students to guess the meaning based on their understanding of the morphemes.

examples

Readology= the study of reading
Subgeology= the study of things under the earth

EXTENSION ACTIVITIES

Give students a list of 4-5 words that share a common morpheme, such as antibiotic, microbiology, symbiotic, and biodegradable. Read the definition aloud for one of the words on the list. Ask students to apply their knowledge of morphemes to identify the word that matches the definition.

7 Sorting

What it's all about

The purpose of sorting is to group words according to relationships or shared features. In a sorting activity, students analyze a list of vocabulary words, search for patterns, and categorize words according to similar attributes. This kind of activity helps students solidify their understanding of conceptual relationships between words.

There are two types of sorting activities: closed and open sorts. In a closed sort the teacher predetermines the categories for sorting the words. In an open sort, students generate their own categories. Marzano et al., (2001) explains that sorting activities — especially those that involve classifying words — provide multiple word exposures and help shape word meanings.

Directions

1. Choose to have students arrange words in a closed or open sort. In a closed sort, the categories will be predetermined; in an open sort, students will create the categories.

2. Provide a list of vocabulary from the unit of study or use words on the Word Wall. If conducting a closed sort, provide the categories into which students will sort the words.

3. Have students work in pairs, or in groups, to sort the words into logical arrangements of two or more. While they sort, students will be using the new vocabulary in conversation.

4. Monitor students as they sort words. Be sure that students are sorting words based on patterns or attributes that contribute to the meaning, rather than on superficial characteristics. For example, encourage students to sort words based on attributes such as definition, relation to an event or process, or part of speech, rather than by simple features such as the same initial letter, number of letters, or number of syllables.

5. Have students share their categories and word lists with the class and discuss other possible formats for sorting.

examples

Closed Sort: Sort the following list of words into groups with the following labels: Shapes, Parts of a Function, Representing Functions, Types of Functions, Included in a Function.

Range	Expression	Formula	Lines	Pairs
Value	Variable	Quadrants	Parabolas	Polynomial
Equality	Graph	Input	f(x)	Vertical Line
Inequality	Continuous	Output	Circles	Test
	X and Y	Domain	Ordered	

EXTENSION ACTIVITY

Select 5 or 6 words from the Word Wall. Have students choose one word that does not belong with the group and explain why it is the odd word out. Continue with the words that are left, again having them choose the odd word out from the remaining words. Ask students to justify their answers as they make their choices. Continue until only two words are left. Next, ask students to explain the relationship between the remaining two words.

graphic organizers

for Vocabulary Words

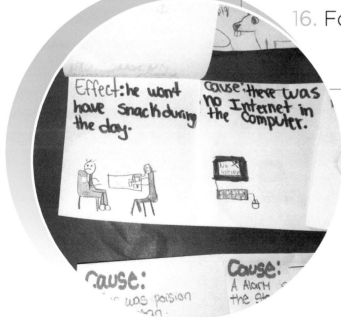

8 Sensory Word Web

(English Language Arts with Extension Activities in Social Studies and Science)

What it's all about

A Sensory Word Web involves the five senses: taste, touch, sight, smell, and hearing. Words like: *large* or *small* express physical characteristics, something than can be seen. Words like: loud or soft describe how something sounds. Words like *scratchy* or *smooth* explain how something feels. Words like *salty* or *bland* are related to taste. Words like *smoky* or *sweet* refer to words associated with smell. Students can brainstorm a list of sensory words on a Word Web – like the one at the right – to preface a writing activity.

Directions

1. Choose a setting like the beach, the desert, a snow-covered mountain, a playground, a soccer field, or a city street. Write the setting of choice in the center circle of a Word Web.

2. Give students five minutes to write any sensory words (taste, touch, see, smell, hear) they associate with the setting on the Word Web. Encourage students to write as many words on each line as possible.

3. Have students brainstorm, collectively, as they compare their notes. Let the list grow as long as suggestions are given.

4. Ask students to write a descriptive paragraph that uses sensory words from the exercise.

5. Have them add 2-3 vocabulary words from the Word Wall to the finished paragraph.

example

taste
thirsty
parched

touch
hot
sizzling

desert

sight
sunny
bright

hear
silence

smell
scorched
dry

EXTENSION ACTIVITIES

For the social studies and science topics listed below, select an event/individual. Have students brainstorm a sensory word web to describe the subject. Then, ask students to describe the scene — in writing — using academic vocabulary from the unit they are studying.

Social Studies: the Underground Railroad, Lincoln's Gettysburg Address, the Dust Bowl, Neil Armstrong walks on the Moon –July 21, 1969

Science: San Francisco earthquakes- 1906 and 1989, Mt. St. Helen's volcano erupts May 18, 1980, Hurricane Katrina in New Orleans, 2005

Word Wall Murals

What it's all about

A mural using Word Wall words is much like a story-board. Based on a unit of study, it provides a visual illustration that advances in several ways. It can be linear, hierarchical, or it can be a collage.

Directions

1. Have students form small groups and provide a piece of chart paper for each group.

2. Provide a concept or target word to each group from a unit of study, and ask students to write the word on the chart paper.

3. Ask students to find computer-generated or printed pictures for the concept or target word and glue them to the chart paper. Students can draw original illustrations as well.

4. Arrange completed charts on the Word Wall in an order, e.g., linear, hierarchical, or collage.

examples

Social Studies: *On a unit called the Road to Revolution, have students add pictures that represent: the Boston Massacre, tyranny, mercantilism, sedition, loyalists, and the Stamp Act.*

English Language Arts: *For a novel, have students add pictures that represent: the rising action, climax, and resolution of the events in the plot.*

Science: *For a unit on weather, have students add pictures that represent: an air mass, front, global conveyor belt, and jet stream.*

Math: *For math, provide a word problem for students to illustrate.*

EXTENSION ACTIVITY

Ask students to walk past the charts on display and add a sentence about the concept that contains one vocabulary word.

Knowledge Rating Scale

What it's all about

The Knowledge Rating Scale can be used to establish prior knowledge of vocabulary before starting a unit of study (Bachowicz & Fisher, 2005).

Directions

1. Read a list of vocabulary words to students. Have them write the words in the first column on the Knowledge Rating Scale.

2. Ask students to mark an X under the next three columns to determine what they know about the word.

3. Put the chart aside until the end of the unit.

4. Return to the chart after completing a unit of study. Ask students who have placed an X in the second or third columns to write a definition or description of the word in the last column.

word	I know this word well.	I've seen/ heard this word, but I'm not sure what it means.	I have never seen this word before.	Now I know the word. it means...
1.				
2.				
3.				
4.				
5.				

examples

Science: *atom, proton, neutron, electron, nucleus*

English Language Arts: *personification, alliteration, hyperbole, plagiarism, rhyme*

Social Studies: *free enterprise, capitalism, entrepreneurship, corporation, stock market*

Math: *linear, perimeter, parallelogram, rhombus, equilateral triangle*

EXTENSION ACTIVITIES

Have students review a personal reading selection using this chart to list new vocabulary words. Ask students to share one new word with the class. Charts can be added to the Word Wall.

11 Word Discovery

What it's all about

The Word Discovery graphic organizer asks students to find context clues and other information in order to communicate personal meaning for a vocabulary word. This kind of organizer can be used to assess student knowledge at the end of a unit of study. Based on the answers students give, word comprehension is obvious.

Directions

1. Distribute the Word Discovery graphic organizers to students, or have them draw a replica.

2. Have students read a section from a unit of study, silently.

3. Have students identify one word they do not understand and enter it into the square in the middle of the graphic.

4. Tell students to complete the graphic organizer by adding the sentence that contained the word, context clues, part of speech, an original sentence, and the definition or description of the word.

5. Place students in groups of three to compare the words they noted on the organizer.

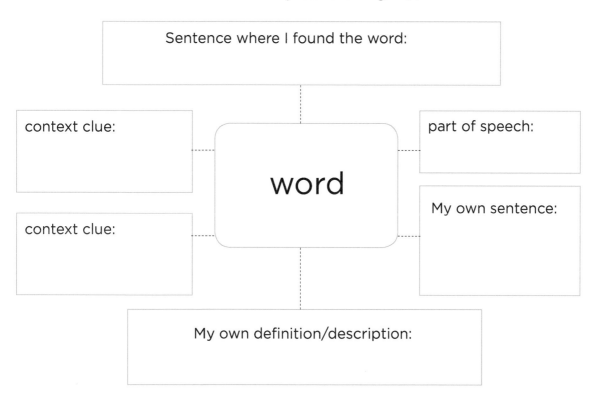

Sentence where I found the word:

context clue:

context clue:

word

part of speech:

My own sentence:

My own definition/description:

example

Sentence Where I Found the Word: A book resting on a table has the force of gravity pulling it toward the earth.

Context Clues: gravity, pulling it toward the earth

Part of Speech: noun

My Own Sentence: Force is just a fancy word for pushing or pulling.

My Own Definition/Description: If I push or pull on something, I am applying force.

EXTENSION ACTIVITY

Have students add a box below the definition (on the graphic organizer) for an illustration of the word.

12 Word Generation

What it's all about

Word Generation allows students to access and note prior knowledge of a vocabulary word very quickly. Students are given a key concept or vocabulary word, and they quickly jot down words that relate to the topic. As students engage in this activity, it is easy for teachers to assess what students already know about a given topic. Teachers can then use prior knowledge to build new knowledge.

Directions

1. Select a key concept or vocabulary word from the text or unit of study.

2. Write the word on the board and ask students to list words related to the target word.

3. Give students one minute to work individually, or in pairs, to brainstorm a list of words.

4. Have students stand and read one word from their list as the teacher records the words on the board. *(Note: The same word may not be given more than once.)* Ask students to circle words on their lists as they are written on the board. When a student has circled all the words on his/her list, he/she should be seated. The last person(s) standing with the longest list is/are the Word Generation champion(s).

5. Conclude the discussion by highlighting information that contributes to understanding the target word and redirect any off-topic words.

examples

Social Studies:

Civil War: North, South, slavery, abolish, Robert E. Lee, Ulysses S. Grant, Abraham Lincoln, cannons, Union, Confederacy, Gettysburg, secession, USA, railroad, Carpetbaggers, Underground Railroad, Harriet Tubman

Math:

variable, linear, term, slope, intercept, x, y, power, constant, access, vertical, horizontal, inequality, percentage

English Language Arts:

personification, hyperbole, rhyme, verse, stanza, repetition, alliteration, point-of-view, imagery, foreshadow, theme, metaphor, simile

Science:

organism, atmospheric, biome, porous, soluble, condensation, metamorphic, sedimentary, nucleus, barometer, volume

12 Word Generation
continued

13 Word Webs

What it's all about

Creating Word Webs with academic vocabulary words gives students multiple exposures to words they will see in science, math, social studies, or English textbooks. By identifying other ways to describe the target word, students are presented with a range of conceptual information.

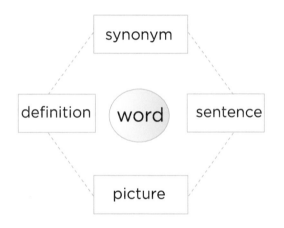

Directions

1. Have students choose one vocabulary word from a recent unit of study.

2. Ask students to use the graphic to define and describe the word with a synonym, definition/description, sentence, and a picture.

example

Word: atmosphere

Definition/Description: earth's air

Sentence: The atmosphere is a mixture of solids and gases, and it surrounds the earth.

Synonym: gaseous envelope

EXTENSION ACTIVITY

Have students complete a sentence stem about the vocabulary word they described on the Word Web, e.g., The more I think about _____, the more I realize...; I wonder about _____ because...; Originally, I thought that _____ meant _____, but now I know it means ... .

14 Four-Corners Word Model (adapted from the Frayer Model, 1969)

What it's all about

The Four-Corners Word Model is an easy, visual way to take vocabulary comprehension to a deeper level of understanding. The model consists of four boxes surrounding a key concept or vocabulary word. The four categories include: simple definition, contextual sentence, visual, and in my own words. Students can write the vocabulary words on an index card; the cards can be assembled; and a personal dictionary is born!

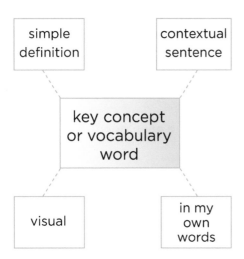

Directions

Steps 1-3 should be completed as a whole class. Steps 4-6 can be completed individually.

1. Using an index card (or vocabulary journal), have students write a vocabulary word, key concept, or key term in the center of the card/page. Tell them to draw a box around the word, similar to the graphic model shown above.

2. From each corner of the boxed term, have students draw a line and a box. In the top right box, have students write a simple definition of the word based on whole class discussion of the word.

3. If students are unfamiliar with the word, have them look up the word in the textbook or in a dictionary. Then, have students craft a simple definition together.

4. In the bottom right box, have students write a contextual sentence, one that expresses the definition of the word. A non-example for the word protagonist would be: *I like the protagonist.* An example would be: *The protagonist in the story was awesome because he defeated the enemy!*

5. In the bottom left box, have students draw a visual of the word, term, or concept.

6. In the top left box, have students put the term in their own words. The example should show that students have an understanding of what the word means. For ELL students, the explanation could be in their native language.

example

simple definition

group of three related things

contextual sentence

The *Lord of the Rings* is part of a trilogy of books written by J.R.R. Tolkien.

trilogy

visual

in my own words

Reading a trilogy means I get to spend lots of time with some of my favorite characters.

EXTENSION ACTIVITY

Have students refer to a dictionary or textbook and write the correct definition on the back of the index card/page. This will give them an academic definition that supports their original work, and it can become part of a personal dictionary.

15 Alphabet Connection

What it's all about

Alphabet Connection allows students to examine their existing knowledge of a key concept or vocabulary word. This process sheds light on what students already know about a given concept, and teachers can use this information to build new knowledge.

A	B	C	D
E	F	G	H
I	J	K	L
M	KEY WORD		N
O	P	Q	R
S	T	U	V
W	X	Y	Z

EXTENSION ACTIVITY

As part of step 6, have groups contribute a definition or description of the word they have given on the Alphabet Connection graphic.

Directions

1. Distribute the Alphabet Connection graphic to students or have them create a page with each letter of the alphabet listed vertically down the left-hand side of a piece of paper.

2. Write the topic or vocabulary term on the board or point to it on the Word Wall.

3. Have students write the word either in the center of the worksheet or on the top of the paper.

4. Ask students to brainstorm (individually) as many words as they can that connect to the key word, using the letters of the alphabet.

5. Have students share their list in pairs and then in groups.

6. Create a master Alphabet Connection with the entire class that is a result of the group work.

example

A amplitude	**B** base binomial	**C** coefficient completing the square complex roots coordinates	**D** domain degree discriminant downward double root dependent variable
E equivalent forms	**F** focus point function factoring	**G** graph grid	**H** horizontal trans
I inverse independent variable imaginary number irrational roots	**J**	**K**	**L** line of symmetry line of directrix
M minimum maximum monomial	**KEY WORD** Quadratic Equation		**N** negative
O ordered pairs	**P** parabola parent function positive prime polynomial	**Q** quadratic formula quadrant	**R** roots range rational
S standard form square root stretching/shrinking scatter plot	**T** trinomial transformation table	**U** upward	**V** vertex vertical trans vertex form variable
W word problem	**X** x-intercept x-axis	**Y** y-intercept y-axis	**Z** zero

16 Foldables

What it's all about

Foldables give students an opportunity to record information about academic vocabulary words. As they work, students write the term and create a visual representation of the word.

Each content area can lend itself to different foldables over time.

Directions

1. Determine 6 - 8 academic vocabulary words that need to be taken to a deeper level of understanding.

2. Distribute a sheet of colored paper to students and have them fold it in half. *(Note: If available, ultra-bright/ florescent paper is a favorite of all students.)*

3. Have students cut one side of the fold into as many slits as needed for the number of words they have.

4. Have students write the word on the front flap, the definition on the back of the front flap, and a picture directly across from the definition.

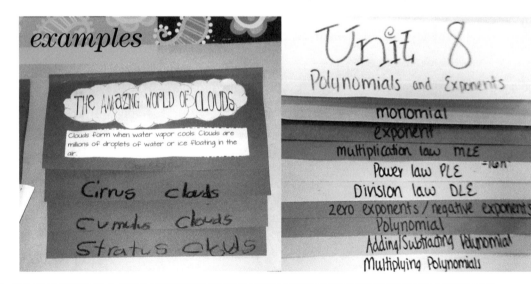

examples

EXTENSION ACTIVITIES

Have students create different types of foldables such as: flip fold, magic square, magic strip, or layered-look book and then share/explain them to a friend.

Vocabulary
words in context

17 Formal/ Informal Pairs

What it's all about

Informal language consists of words that are easily understood; it is used in friendly conversations or among family members. Formal language is used in textbooks, classrooms, and businesses; it usually does not contain contractions or personal pronouns.

Learning the difference between formal and informal language helps students incorporate more academic language into classroom discussions and writing.

Directions

1. Provide sentence strips with corresponding pairs of statements written in formal and informal English. Distribute one sentence to each individual or small group of students. For example: (1) All students are invited to an after-school movie today at 3:00. (2) Hey, want to go to the movie?

2. Ask students to identify the sentence they have been given as formal or informal language.

3. Ask students to walk around the classroom and share their sentences with other students. Ask them to stop when they find their partner sentence.

4. Have student groups share their corresponding sentences with the class.

5. Have students check to see if they have identified the sentence correctly, i.e., formal/informal.

example

Humans maintain homeostasis by shivering because muscle movement generates heat that keeps body temperature at 98.6°.

People shiver to keep warm so their body will stay at 98.6°.

EXTENSION ACTIVITY

To help students see the difference between formal and informal language, have them translate the formal language used in a section/chapter of a textbook into a simple, informal sentence they can share with a friend.

Brick and Mortar Words

What it's all about

There are two types of academic vocabulary words: *brick* and *mortar*. Dutro & Moran (2003) refer to brick and mortar words as a way to discern between content-specific vocabulary and general academic language. Brick words are in bold print in a textbook, and they are listed in the glossary. Mortar words are general academic language, and as the name implies, mortar words hold language together.

BRICK WORDS:

Brick words are specific to the content and concepts studied in class, and they have to be taught directly. The table to the right shows brick words across subject areas.

Reading/ Language Arts	*irony* *theme* *foreshadowing* *internal conflict*
Social Studies	*emancipation* *democracy* *manifest destiny*
Math	*reciprocal* *quadratic equation* *polygons*
Science	*meiosis* *gravity* *biodiversity*

EXTENSION ACTIVITY

Give students a list of three brick words and 10-12 mortar words. Have students connect the brick words with the mortar words to make a sentence.

18 Brick and Mortar Words
continued

MORTAR WORDS: Mortar words are general academic words that can be found in textbooks, conversations, or texts across all subject areas. Mortar words hold academic language together in sentences. They include transitional words like *because*, signal words like *first* or *second*, and test-specific language like *best represents* or *based upon*. Mortar words are often abstract, and sometimes, they do not have a clear definition. The best way for students to learn these words is by using them. Mortar words allow students to put complex and formal structures together when communicating, and mortar words hold brick words together. The table above shows mortar words across subject areas. *(Note: Mortar words could easily be used in all content areas, depending on the context. For example, the word balance could be used in math when referring to an equation, but it could also apply to a balance of power in social studies.)*

Reading/ Language Arts	*conveys* *reflects* *persuade* *punctuation*	*contains* *best represents* *narrate* *whereas*
Social Studies	*consequently* *consists of* *contributed*	*therefore* *implications*
Math	*rreasonable* *calculate* *equals* *isolate*	*derive* *believe* *balance*
Science	*consequently* *sustainability* *function*	*dependent* *balance*

Understanding **brick** and **mortar** terms is vital to student success in vocabulary development because it leads to academic success.

Directions

1. Divide students into groups.

2. Choose 3 brick words and 7-9 mortar words. Write each word on a separate index card.

3. Place the cards in an envelope and give each group an envelope.

4. Have students create a sentence using a combination of the brick and mortar words.

example

| Alliteration | occurs | mostly | in | poetry |

| but | sometimes | it | is | used | in |

| narrative | writing. |

Highlight and Replace

What it's all about

One of the best indicators of student understanding is the ability to use essential vocabulary when speaking about a topic. In this activity, students have the opportunity to supply synonyms, antonyms, and descriptions for the words they are working with in class. As they do, teachers can readily tell when students have a good grasp of the words they are studying.

Directions

1. Select two reading passages for students. The passages can be the introduction to the next unit of study, or they can be short sections from a unit being studied.

2. Highlight vocabulary words in the passage that students need to know to complete this unit of study. *(Note: Mortar words should not be highlighted. For a definition of mortar words, see page 40.)*

3. Place students in groups, and have them read the passages to each other without reading the highlighted words. Instead, when students come to a highlighted word, they should provide a description, synonym, or antonym that describes the word.

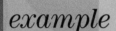

example

MAJOR MITCHELL, THE LEADER OF THE FIFTH REGIMENT OF REDCOATS, wrestled his horse while he tried to gain control of the situation. The stallion struggled against the tautness of the reins, but settled momentarily.

"Fix bayonets!" Major Mitchell ordered, and his

EXTENSION ACTIVITY

To make this a real-life activity, have students choose an article from a favorite magazine or Internet source. Ask them to bring the passage to class to read to a shoulder partner. Have them follow the same procedure of highlighting and replacing words for their partners.

oral vocabulary

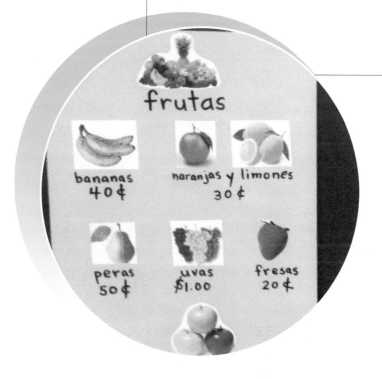

20 Vocal Vocabulary
(English Language Arts, Social Studies, and Science)

What it's all about

Vocal Vocabulary asks students to probe the definition of a word by writing and telling a story that makes the definition of a word very clear. As the story is told, students practice their speaking skills.

Directions

1. Ask students to select a vocabulary word from a lesson or from the Word Wall. Make sure students have a definition or clear description of the word as they begin this exercise.

2. Have students search their memories and experiences to find a time that relates to or is an example of the word they choose. The stories they recall can be personal or second-hand.

3. Have students begin the story with this sentence stem: I have chosen the word _____ for my story because it reminds me of the time _____.

4. Tell students to write one paragraph that explains the word. (See example on the next page.) Remind students that a well-written story will make the definition of the word very clear to the listener.

5. Have students assemble in groups and take turns telling their stories.

6. After students tell their stories, have group members give one compliment.

EXTENSION ACTIVITIES

Skip steps 5 & 6, and have students use their stories for the Inside/Outside Circle on p. 46.

Have students make a list of the Vocal Vocabulary words used by their group members. Ask students to write a sentence using each of the words presented in the group stories. If the stories were clear, students will be able to write sentences that allow the teacher to assess mastery of the words.

example

SOCIAL STUDIES

"I have chosen the word **deluge** for my story because it reminds me of the time I babysat for my younger brother. While we were having a snack together, he spilled chocolate ice cream all over his shirt. I told him to bring his shirt to the sink in the kitchen. I knew I would have to wash it. But, before I could do that, the phone rang. It was my very best friend from school, and before I knew it, we had chatted for fifteen minutes. I told her I really had to go and take care of my brother. We said goodbye, and I went to wash my brother's stained shirt. On my way to the kitchen, I could see a flash flood was headed my way. Oh, no! When I got to the sink, there was my brother....on his little step stool... running water on his shirt. The water was streaming over the side and had been for some time. "Look," he said, "almost all of the ice cream is gone." He seemed pleased with himself, but now my job was to clean up the water really fast before mom and dad came home."

21 Inside/Outside Circle

What it's all about

This activity facilitates student conversation using vocabulary words (Kagan, 1990). While students stand in concentric circles, facing one another, they participate in short, guided discussions or reviews with a partner.

Directions

1. Ask students to form two concentric circles facing one another, an inside circle and an outside circle.

2. Provide one vocabulary word for each student on the inside circle.

3. Ask the "inside" circle students to define and describe the vocabulary word to the person standing opposite them in the outside circle.

4. Have the "outside" circle students use the word in an original sentence. *(Note: For math words, students can use the terms in a quiz-like fashion.)* When the sentence has been articulated, tell students to get ready to move.

5. Have students in the outside circle rotate one person to the right while the inside circle remains still. All students will now have a new partner, and the activity can be repeated (Kagan, 1990).

EXTENSION ACTIVITIES

Have students share their stories from Vocal Vocabulary (p. 44) with a partner.

Give students one prefix, such as *un*. Have them think of a word that begins with the prefix and ask them to tell it to their partner. Have students record the words as they rotate in the Inside/Outside Circle.

22 Voice Mail Greetings

(English Language Arts, Social Studies, and Science)

What it's all about

Voice mail greetings can be many things... dull, creative, interesting, and even informative. While writing this activity, students get the chance to recall a figure from history, science, or reading to create the voice mail greeting they might have heard, should that person have voice mail.

Directions

1. Brainstorm a list of figures from any content area, e.g., Abraham Lincoln, Gregor Mendel, Louis Pasteur, Edgar Allan Poe, Shel Silverstein, Marie Curie, Galileo, Thomas Edison, Susan B. Anthony, Davy Crockett, Jackie Robinson, Christopher Columbus, Rick Riordan.

2. In pairs, have students choose one person and note his/her characteristics. For example, Abraham Lincoln was: honest, fair, tall, and a remarkable leader.

3. Based on the characteristics students have brainstormed, have them create the Voice Mail Greeting they might hear should they contact that person. Tell students to use at least two vocabulary words in the greeting.

examples

English Language Arts: *Hello, this is Shel Silverstein. Please leave a message of* **significant** *importance — possibly in poem form — like the ones you might have* **perused** *in my book* Where the Sidewalk Ends. *Here's an example called Early Bird: "Oh, if you're a bird, be an early bird/And catch the worm for your breakfast plate./If you're a bird, be an early, early bird. /But if you're a worm, sleep late."*

Social Studies: *Hello, This is Abraham Lincoln. If you are courageous,* **trustworthy,** *and* **tenacious,** *I'd like to* **converse** *with you about some very important issues. Please leave a message. If not, please call General McLellan.*

Science: *You have reached Galileo. They call me the father of modern* **observational** *astronomy, and perhaps that is the reason you called. If so, please* **pose** *your question, and I will respond soon.*

EXTENSION ACTIVITY

Have students look at the Word Wall and choose at least two vocabulary words to use in the greeting.

Voice Cards

What it's all about

Newly acquired vocabulary terms can often be difficult to pronounce. By using different voices and saying academic words in multiple fashions, the somewhat intimidating vocabulary term becomes much more manageable. Creating Voice Cards is a fun way to practice the pronunciation of academic vocabulary. Sometimes, humor facilitates a way to make new words part of a student's permanent lexicon.

Directions

1. Have students brainstorm different moods, voices, situations, settings, or people to use when pronouncing new academic vocabulary words.

2. Have students use their brainstorming list to make different index cards. For example: riding in a bumpy car, talking into a fan, the President, a rapper, a rock star, riding on a roller coaster, freezing cold, sultry, a specific teacher, or Mickey Mouse.

3. Have them punch holes in each card and put the cards on a ring.

4. Choose 6-8 academic vocabulary words to use when practicing pronunciation. List the words on the board or highlight them on the Word Wall.

5. Form groups of four.

6. Have students use their Voice Cards to dictate how to say each word.

7. Ask students to go around the table pronouncing the words as indicated on the index card…but students should not choose their own voice. Instead, have the person on the left decide the way the next person will say the word.

8. Each person will pronounce the word in different voices before moving to a new word.

examples

happy	excited	pinched nose	riding on a bumpy road
roller coaster	opera singer	rap star	sultry
in a hurry	Mickey Mouse	frustrated	depressed
giggly	robot	blissful	silly
monster	toddler	talking into a fan	freezing cold

EXTENSION ACTIVITIES

As students pronounce the words multiple times by multiple methods, have them say the definition or create a contextual sentence using the different Voice Cards.

writing with vocabulary words

24 Cloze Exercises

What it's all about

A cloze exercise is a text or a reading passage that is missing words. Cloze exercises focus on contextual cueing, strengthen a reader's ability to anticipate text, and expand confidence in reading.

Teachers can prepare cloze activities for students in different ways. For example, to study text from any subject area, choose a passage and delete key content area terms or academic words from the text. Insert blank lines where the word was written. Or, teachers can create their own cloze exercises by writing stories using the vocabulary words from classroom study.

Directions

1. Choose a text or excerpt from a textbook, magazine, newspaper article, or Internet source.

2. Delete content area terms to focus on academic vocabulary.

3. Delete transitional words from the text to focus on cueing skills.

4. Provide a word bank (a list of the words next to each paragraph) for students to use to fill in the blanks.

example

WORD BANK

wrangle

decreed

jostling

vigil

discordant

reverted

adage

plaudits

bonanza

preclude

churlish

Since we knew tickets to the concert were scarce, we arrived at the ticket office at 4:00 a.m. and kept a _vigil_, waiting for hours for the office to open. Nothing would _preclude_ or prevent us from getting those tickets!

As the hours passed, the sun rose, and a crowd began to gather. There was some pushing and _jostling_, and soon people in the crowd became rude and _churlish_. I wouldn't be surprised if some of those groups at the end of the line began to _wrangle_ with each other. After all, they were already arguing about who was first in line.

The office finally opened, and the crowd offered its _plaudits_ as they clapped loudly. I guess you know the old _adage_, "the early bird catches the worm." Since we were first in line, we moved up and purchased our tickets quickly. With the tickets safely in our hands, we felt like we had won a _bonanza_. They were so valuable!

We _reverted_ back to our car through the ever-growing crowd. This was not an easy thing to do, but as we reached the parking lot, we _decreed_, "We had a great day and can't wait to see the concert." Not a _discordant_ note was heard in our car the entire way home!

example

WORD BANK

equal

score

consecrate

liberty

increased

battlefield

perish

dedicated

Four _____ and seven years ago our fathers brought forth on this continent, a new nation, conceived in _____, and dedicated to the proposition that all men are created _____.

Now we are engaged in a great civil war, testing whether that nation, or any nation so conceived and so dedicated, can long endure. We are met on a great _____ of that war. We have come to dedicate a portion of that field, as a final resting place for those who here gave their lives that that nation might live. It is altogether fitting and proper that we should do this.

But, in a larger sense, we cannot dedicate, we cannot _____, we cannot hallow, this ground. The brave men, living and dead, who struggled here, have consecrated it, far above our poor power to add or detract. The world will little note, nor long remember what we say here, but it can never forget what they did here. It is for us the living, rather, to be _____ here to the unfinished work which they who fought here have thus far so nobly advanced. It is rather for us to be here dedicated to the great task remaining before us—that from these honored dead we take _____ devotion to that cause for which they gave the last full measure of devotion—that we here highly resolve that these dead shall not have died in vain—that this nation, under God, shall have a new birth of freedom—and that government of the people, by the people, for the people, shall not perish from the earth.

Abraham Lincoln, Gettysburg Address, 1863

EXTENSION ACTIVITY

After students have completed their cloze exercises, have them create an original cloze activity using vocabulary words from a recent unit of study. Ask them to exchange with a partner. In pairs, have them complete the cloze activity their partners wrote.

Roaming Paragraphs

What it's all about

The Roaming (or Roving) Paragraph does just that... it moves throughout the classroom. Building on a starter sentence, students add to a story using other vocabulary words.

Directions

1. Arrange students in groups of five. Assign five vocabulary words to each group, with each student receiving a different word.

2. Have all students write one starter sentence using their new vocabulary word. Ask students to underline the word in the starter sentence and place their initials at the end of the sentence.

3. Have students pass the sentence to the right.

4. Ask students to add a second sentence, adding their word in a sentence that continues the thought/idea already started. Now, there will be two sentences (their own and their partner's) with one vocabulary word each.

5. Have students add their initials and pass the two sentences to the right.

6. Ask students to add one more sentence using their vocabulary word. Continue until all group members have had a chance to add to the paragraphs.

7. Upon completion, there will be a short paragraph with five sentences containing five different vocabulary words.

EXTENSION ACTIVITY

Have students write one sentence using a vocabulary word. Have them switch papers with students in their groups of five to see how others have used their vocabulary words. *(Note: Students can initial the sentences they read.)* Next, have students return to their original sentences and continue to write two more sentences (using two new words) with the ideas they have collected from their group members.

Narrative/ Procedural Writing

What it's all about

Teachers in all content areas are responsible for developing students who can write well. Someday, those students may become scientists, historians, or mathematicians who will be responsible for producing various types of writing, narrative and procedural. Therefore, writing with vocabulary from the content area helps students focus and use academic vocabulary on a deeper level.

To practice Narrative/Procedural Writing, teachers should select the writing format that best lends itself to the content being taught. Typically, a narrative style works best with English language arts and history, while procedural writing works well with science and math. However, with a little creativity and flexibility, a teacher could feasibly incorporate either style. As always, modeling the activity helps students before they tackle the task on their own.

Directions

1. Select the writing format (narrative or procedural) and topic that will best satisfy your content objective.

2. Tell students they will be writing either a narrative or a procedural explanation which incorporates specific content vocabulary.

3. Model the process before asking students to work independently.

4. Provide a list of 4-5 academic vocabulary words for students to incorporate into their writing.

5. Ask students to think of a meaningful way to connect the vocabulary they have been given into a narrative or procedural explanation. Have students work individually for five minutes to brainstorm a bulleted list of their ideas. At the end of five minutes, ask students to get together with a partner.

6. Allow students to share their ideas and to ask for suggestions from their partners. Give them a two-minute time allotment as they work with partners.

7. Restart the timer for 15-25 minutes (if time allows) and have students write a draft of the narrative/procedural explanation. Circulate around the room during this time to encourage students and to help anyone who might be having difficulty. Let students know when only three minutes are left. At this point, ask them to bring their writing to a conclusion.

8. Students can share their writing in small groups.

examples

English Language Arts: *Write a fable or fairytale.*

Science: *Explain a formula.*

Math: *Explain how to solve a problem to another student.*

Social Studies: *Write a letter to your cousin explaining what happened at the Battle of San Jacinto.*

EXTENSION ACTIVITIES

For Narrative Writing: Have students trade papers with a partner and write a response/review to the other person's narrative.

For Procedural Writing (groups): Have small groups of students work together to solve a problem described in the writing.

For Procedural Writing (individually): Have students write a procedural explanation — that includes academic vocabulary — to show how they solved a problem. Have students share their written work in small groups.

27 Targeted Ticket Out

What it's all about

In a quick, direct activity, students write about the academic focus of the day's lesson on a sticky note, called a Targeted Ticket Out.

Not only is this an opportunity for students to stay focused until the very end of class, but it reinforces and assesses student knowledge. As students write their sticky notes, the vocabulary used in class that day is reinforced. As teachers collect the notes, they have a chance to assess student grasp of the lesson content. Most importantly, it provides a way for teachers to tailor the next day's lesson.

This kind of activity is often called a "sponge activity" because it "soaks up" those few extra minutes at the end of class. In a very practical way, it gives students a chance to absorb recently introduced vocabulary words as they use them in writing (Marzano, 2004).

Directions

1. Distribute a sticky note to students five minutes before class ends. Ask students to jot down what they learned during class today — in a minimum of 15 words. Remind students to focus their response on the vocabulary words they learned during class today.

2. Provide several starter sentences, as needed, for students to use, e.g., Today, I learned_____. I think_____. Tomorrow, I hope to find out_____.

3. Stand by the door and collect a sticky note from students as they leave class.

4. Read and use student responses to guide tomorrow's lesson.

examples

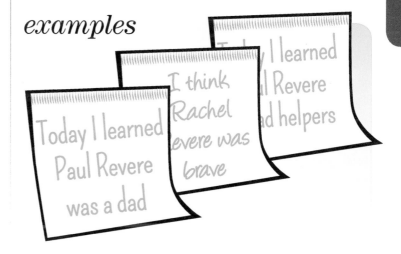

EXTENSION ACTIVITY

Choose 3-4 Targeted Ticket Out sticky notes to model the next day. Two should be excellent examples; two should require revisions. Write them on the board for students to see when they come to class. Ask students if all the vocabulary words have been used correctly. If not, ask how they should be rewritten.

28 Text Conversation

What it's all about

This is something many students love to do...write notes to each other via text. In this activity, there is one requirement and that is to use vocabulary words from the Word Wall.

Directions

1. Give students a paper outline of a cell phone screen or have them sketch a drawing of their own.

2. Target two vocabulary words for students to use as they complete this activity.

3. Brainstorm the characteristics of a writer or important figure studied in class. This person could be from any content area, e.g., Hans Christian Andersen, Louisa May Alcott, Thomas Edison, Pythagoras, or Martin Luther King, Jr. *(Note: For math, text conversations might be about how to solve a problem.)*

4. Have one student take the role of the character/figure. Have the other student ask questions.

5. In pairs, have students write notes in the form of a text, passing them back and forth as they finish each entry. *(Note: Tell students to use a minimum of twenty words in each text. In addition, ask them to include two vocabulary words in their text conversation.)* After five minutes, ask students to stop writing.

6. Take time to read some samples and discuss the way vocabulary words help convey the message. *(Note: If some vocabulary words are used awkwardly or incorrectly, model ways to work with the words so they are used with more fluency.)*

example

> Marie Antoinette, did you really say "let them eat cake?"

> No, that was a rumor made up by people who didn't like me.

EXTENSION ACTIVITIES

Choose a second character from each content area, e.g., Marie Pasteur, Rick Riordan, Susan B. Anthony, or Albert Einstein. Have students play the role of one figure as they text to the other. Points of view of each character/figure should be evident.

29 Writing Roulette

What it's all about

Writing Roulette is a creative writing strategy, and like the game of roulette, random writing sections can produce prize-winning creations. Used to reinforce vocabulary knowledge and to incorporate newly acquired academic vocabulary, this activity allows students to explore thoughts freely without the limitations and constraints of grammar and mechanics.

Directions

1. Group students into triads. Explain that they will be working individually and then together to create a written work. Tell students that each person will create part of a three-part story.

2. Provide a three-part framework for writing that is best suited to the particular content area. For example, an English language arts teacher may choose: 1) setting and characters, 2) problem, and 3) resolution.

3. Tell students they have 3-5 minutes to write each of the three sections. Ask them to use at least one academic vocabulary word in each section, and have them underline the words they use. Set the timer for 3-5 minutes for the first part of the story framework, in this case the setting and characters. *(Note: It is important for teachers to write with students, to model the process of "quick writing.")*

4. Have students switch papers with the person on the left when the timer sounds. Ask students to read what their partner wrote. Then, have them add to the story by creating the second part of the story framework, the problem. Again, set the timer for 3-5 minutes.

5. Allow the story to rotate within the group by having students switch once more with the person on the left.

6. Give students time to read the two sections, and then have them complete the story by writing the third part, the resolution. Give students 5-6 minutes for this part of the activity.

7. When time is up, have students switch papers. Students should now have their original work in their hands. Of course, it will have two more sections added to it!

8. Allow students time to read the story silently, and then time to share the story within the triad.

Writing Roulette
continued

Encourage students to spend time revising the written work completed by their triad, this time taking a close look at grammar/mechanics and spelling.

Provide students with a list of current academic vocabulary words, similar to an anticipation guide. Challenge students to use all of the words in order, using the Writing Roulette strategy format. For example, if there are six vocabulary words listed, the first student will incorporate the first two words in writing; the second student will use the next two words; and the third student will use the last two words.

Instead of completing Writing Roulette within a triad, have students get up when the timer sounds, walk around class, and exchange their writing with another student. The end result will be a completed story, as it is in the original activity, but this technique appeals to the kinesthetic student.

30 Children's Vocabulary Book

What it's all about

The more students use the new vocabulary words they read in their textbooks, the more they will internalize them. In this project — applying vocabulary words in an original children's book — students make new vocabulary words part of their repertoire. This project can and should take place over a period of time, depending on the levels and abilities of students. Vocabulary from the units studied in class and on the Word Wall should be incorporated in the work. Students may work in pairs to complete this project. This activity can be completed in all content areas.

Directions

1. Read several children's books, related to your content area. Suggestions for Social Studies: *The Wall* by Eve Bunting, *The Story of Ruby Bridges* by Robert Coles, *Faithful Elephants* by Yukio Tsuchiya, *From Lanterns to Liberty*, by Bill Perryman and Marguerite Hartill. For English Language Arts: *Gila Monsters Meet You at the Airport* by Marjorie Weinman Sharmat, *Alexander and the Terrible, Horrible, No Good, Very Bad Day,* by Judith Viorst. For Science: *The Great Kapok Tree* by Lynne Cherry, *Just a Dream* by Chris Van Allsburg. For Math: *Sir Cumference and the Off-the-Charts Dessert* by C. Neuschwander, *Ten, Nine, Eight* by Molly Bang.

2. Discuss the characteristics of children's books, e.g, short text on each page, illustrations, a story that develops and concludes in a limited number of pages, a recognizable theme, etc.

3. Have students brainstorm a list of ideas they might want to use as the topic of an original children's book. To start brainstorming, suggest that students think of something that happened when they were younger, something they disliked doing but learned to like, or something they discovered about a friend.

4. Ask students to write a few paragraphs in rough draft form for the book. *(Note: The story should be approximately 150-200 words long (4-5 paragraphs), and it should include 3-5 vocabulary words.)* Encourage students to create stories based on their brainstorming notes. Tell them to look back at their notes periodically for ideas, and explain that those ideas may spark new ideas. Remind them to jot down new thoughts, as these can be quickly forgotten.

5. Explain that rough drafts are exactly that….rough, unpolished, and unfinished. Tell students that when they revise a rough draft, they will see the work take shape. One of the first steps in revision is to have students look at the Word Wall in the classroom and choose 2-3 words to insert in the text. Students may have to manipulate the words to get a good fit, but this helps them become better writers. Students can experiment with sentence variety, repetition, or dialogue as they make revisions.

6. Have students gather together in small groups to read their drafts and ask for feedback from the group members. Remind students to incorporate the feedback when revising their work.

7. Review the way a children's book is separated into many pages with short text on each page. Have students note where to separate the sentences/paragraphs they have written so they can become the pages for a children's book.

8. Have students illustrate the pages and prepare a cover. Illustrations can be drawn by hand, computer-generated, or clipped from a magazine.

examples

Alligators seem to walk **audaciously** along the river bank.

Bears **bask** in the bright sun by the blue bay.

Why do cute cats **cower** in the corner?

Dynamic dogs perform in dog shows.

Exotic elephants eat everything edible.

Flamingos **flaunt** their famous pink feathers in front of their fans.

EXTENSION ACTIVITY

Have students share their books with others in the class setting, with parents or younger siblings, or with students in the elementary school.

Have students write an ABC children's book using vocabulary words.

using vocabulary creatively

31 Vocabulary Sale

What it's all about

When new vocabulary words are introduced to students, the words serendipitously pop up in TV commercials, books, magazines, or advertisements. The newly-learned word triggers a memory in the subconscious and tells the brain that it knows that word. Meta-cognitively speaking, there is a familiarity that was not there before, and attention is paid. Often, the word is an intrinsic part of an advertisement like the one in the sample below.

Directions

1. Have students choose one vocabulary word from this week's lessons.

2. Ask students to invent a product using that word as the name of the product. Have them describe the product in a short paragraph using three other vocabulary words.

3. Tell students they can illustrate the advertisement.

4. Post sample vocabulary ads on the Word Wall for all to see.

example

Are there some unwanted guests at your backyard party? You know those pesky mosquitoes who don't make their presence known until you say, "Ouch!" To <u>preclude</u> their visits, try Oust Bug Spray. This <u>concentrated</u> lotion will keep you comfortable and pest-free. The product is all-natural and promises to send those uninvited guests to distant <u>locales.</u>

EXTENSION ACTIVITY

Have students clip an advertisement from a magazine or newspaper that uses a vocabulary word they have just learned. Ask them to underline the word. Place it on the Word Wall.

32 Haiku

What it's all about

Haikus are a Japanese form of poetry consisting of three lines — five syllables in the first and third lines, and seven syllables in the second line.

In this exercise, students write a haiku to practice a word's definition. Correct use of a vocabulary word in a haiku lets the teacher assess knowledge of the word.

Haikus can be written about words from any content area. Sometimes, haikus can be humorous, and often, humor is a great way for students to retain information.

Directions

1. Tell students that vocabulary words can be used creatively. Vocabulary words don't always have to be part of a report or an essay.

2. Explain the structure of a haiku –three lines, constructed with a 5-7-5 syllable format, in the respective lines.

3. Have students choose a word or select a word for them and have them write a haiku.

examples

MATH
A **cryptic** problem
Rankled my brain for hours
Needed to solve it.

SOCIAL STUDIES
Thomas Edison
Oh so many inventions
Electricity.

SCIENCE
The **gravity** on
Earth pulls on each of us so
We don't float away.

ENGLISH LANGUAGE ARTS
Driven swiftly by
two characters, the plot can
Reach its **conclusion**.

EXTENSION ACTIVITY

To allow students to experiment with vocabulary words in more creative ways, have them write an extended metaphor using a vocabulary word. For example:

Epitaph
The end of eternity, carved in stone,
Cold, gray, and lifeless.
Stands quietly like a rigid soldier
On call forever.

Organize a reading for students to share their work. Students can perform for the entire class, or they can work in small groups.

Add haikus to a Word Wall.

33 Acrostics

What it's all about

An acrostic is a series of lines in which the first letters of each line form a word, and eventually the order forms a verse. By writing acrostics, students engage in a simple activity that allows them to dig deeper into the meaning of any given vocabulary word. This activity gives students multiple exposures to vocabulary words, and words can be chosen from any content area.

Directions

1. Group students homogeneously for this activity.

2. Select a vocabulary word for students; have them choose a word from their lists; or have them select a word from the Word Wall.

3. Have students write each letter of the word on the left margin of a piece of paper.

4. Ask students to write a phrase or a sentence for each letter. Tell students that each phrase/sentence should help define the word. Provide examples for students, as needed. (See examples below.)

examples

English Language Arts:

The story I read yesterday
Had a message for
Everyone because
My author wanted
Each reader to learn something
　　important from the story.

Social Studies:

Looking to order
A society
Washington and others
Set up rules to live by

Math:

Various
Algebraic expressions
Represent
Individual numbers
Alphabetically
By labeling
Each changeable letter

Science:

Everything equal, an
　　imaginary line dividing
Quantities of continents
　　and oceans
Unusually
Awesome
Topography
Of northern and
　　southern hemispheres
Right here on earth

EXTENSION ACTIVITY

Students can illustrate their acrostics in a way that makes the definition even clearer.

Acrostics can be added to a Word Wall.

34 Comic Strips (English Language Arts, Social Studies, and Science)

What it's all about

Comic Strips give students an opportunity to use vocabulary words in context. In addition, they reinforce the meaning of words by associating them with visual representations.

To create a comic strip, students craft a cartoon that incorporates academic vocabulary in a logical manner.

Directions

1. Select a few comic strips from the newspaper to use as models for students. (If possible, choose some that have vocabulary words in the text.) Share them aloud in class. Ask students to describe the unique characteristics of a comic strip, e.g., dialogue; frames; the use of pictures to portray action, feelings, emotion; play on words; humor, etc.

2. Distribute 3 index cards to each student, one for each frame of the cartoon.

3. Have students incorporate this week's vocabulary words into a vocabulary comic strip that is three frames long.

4. Remind students that the comic strip should have a clear beginning, middle, and end, and it should incorporate the elements they identified when reading the model comic strips.

5. Students can share their work in small groups and then place their Comic Strips on the Word Wall.

example

EXTENSION ACTIVITY

Have students shuffle their index cards and trade them with partners. Have partners sequence the cards chronologically.

35 Illustrated Text

What it's all about

Illustrating text not only facilitates word learning, idea forming, and problem solving, but it promotes met cognition. Marzano et al., (2001) includes constructing visuals and symbolic representations as effective tenets of vocabulary instruction. With these principles as a foundation, students can connect to vocabulary in context by creating nonlinguistic representations such as sketches, pictures, diagrams, symbols, or designs. This activity works well in all content areas, especially math.

Directions

1. Have students fold a sheet of paper lengthwise in order to form two columns. Ask students to label the left side: *Written Text*. Have them label the right side: *Illustrated Text*.

2. Have students copy, verbatim, sections of a text (in the left column) that contain target vocabulary words in context. In the right column, have students create a visual that illustrates the target word.

3. Instruct students to fold their papers in half, so that only the illustrations are showing. Pair them with another student who will use the visual cues as a guide for defining and retelling.

example

The rider quickly turned the mare and headed in the opposite direction at a full gallop.

EXTENSION ACTIVITY

Have students cut the paper lengthwise to separate the two columns, and then cut apart each recorded text selection and each illustration. Pair them with a new partner who will match the illustrations to the corresponding text.

vocabulary games

36 Online Flashcards

What it's all about

Today's students are hardwired into technology. To take advantage of the technology mindset, simple online flashcards and vocabulary games can provide multiple opportunities for students to encounter content area vocabulary. The flashcards and games can be created by the teacher or by students.

Many schools provide teacher logins for access to websites that make it easy for teachers to create puzzles, games, and flashcards in relatively little time. However, there is an abundance of free sites online as well, and they are just a click away.

To sample some of the websites available and to create online flashcards. try:

flashcardstash.com
quizlet.com
flashcardmachine.com

Directions

1. Create a login on the website of choice, and follow the simple steps to create your own online flashcards or puzzles.

2. Allow students to review online flashcards or play online games independently or in pairs.

3. Have students work in pairs, taking turns answering questions and keeping track of how many correct responses were given.

example

Impromptu

unrehearsed, unprepared

EXTENSION ACTIVITY

Students can study anywhere when they create their own flashcards on their tablets or mobile phones with free flashcard apps such as Flashcards+ or Flashcardlet.

Crossword Puzzles

What it's all about

The educational value of crossword puzzles is readily apparent when the skills to complete them are considered. Varied skills like spelling, definitions, word analysis, word comprehension, reasoning, memory, and recall take center stage when solving a crossword puzzle. All of these skills offer multiple opportunities for students to learn words.

Crossword puzzles can be used to introduce a unit of study, or they can be used to assess knowledge of words already studied. Crossword puzzles can be used across all content areas.

There are many online sites that allow teachers to create crossword puzzles for free, such as:
www.puzzle-maker.com/CW/
www.puzzle-maker.com/
www.discoveryeducation.com/free-puzzlemaker

Directions

1. Give students instructions for completing a crossword puzzle. If students have never completed a crossword, tell them to start the puzzle by reading the first across clue, look for the number on the puzzle, and fill in the answer.

2. Tell students not to be concerned if an answer is not readily apparent. Instead, encourage students to move on to the next clue. Explain that the clues can be read and answered randomly, if need be. Tell students that often the answer to the next clue reveals the answer to one that had been missed along the way.

3. Be sure to tell students that some answers have more than one word, and there are no spaces between words in a crossword puzzle.

EXTENSION ACTIVITIES

For higher level crosswords, write clues that are not merely a definition. Instead, write clues that suggest recall of the correct answer. Or, write clues that give examples of the answer. For example, a symbol in math is x.

Have students search the newspaper or a favorite magazine to find a crossword they can complete.

Have students create a crossword based on their favorite sport or hobby.

Crossword Puzzles

continued

example

DIRECTIONS: Use the following words to help you complete this crossword puzzle.

> revolution, Colonist, liberty, allegiance, loyalty, Parliament, engraving, Patriot, express rider, Buckman's Tavern, Lexington Green, Redcoats, Regulars, militiamen, Sons of Liberty, silversmith, treason

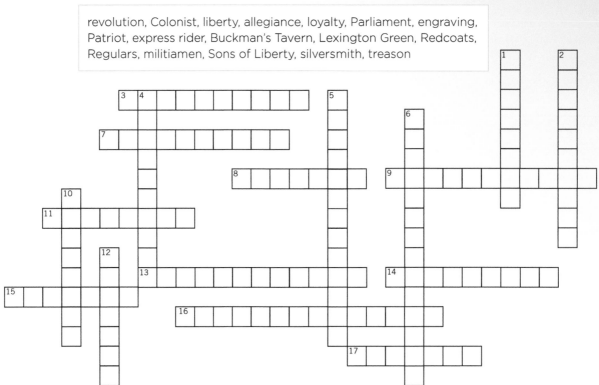

ACROSS

3. the legislature of Great Britain
7. men serving in the army or militia
8. being disloyal or betraying one's country or government
9. a person who makes or repairs articles of silver
11. soldiers of the British army during the American Revolution
13. a messenger, usually traveling in haste to carry important news
14. a design on a metal plate or block of wood used to make copies
15. being faithful to a government or to a person
16. a place where militiamen gathered after training sessions; the place where John Hancock left his trunk
17. freedom from foreign rule; independence

DOWN

1. a person who settled in the American colonies
2. the overthrow of an established government or political system
4. the loyalty of a citizen to his/her government
5. a secretive group that opposed the Stamp Act and were concerned with protecting the rights and liberties of the American Colonists
6. the spot where Revere heard the shot heard round the world
10. an alternate name for the Redcoats
12. a person who supports his country with great devotion

Pict-o-Words

What it's all about

In this mnemonic strategy, students construct word pictures that connect vocabulary words with visuals. The actual vocabulary word is incorporated in the visual clue, making it part of the context. In Marzano and Pickering's Six-Step Vocabulary Teaching Process (2005), he states that pictographs — or symbolic representations of a term — give students multiple exposures to words, helps them connect a word to its meaning, and aids in recall.

Directions

1. Randomly assign a vocabulary word to each student or a small group of students.

2. Give students two sticky notes and a notecard (or a blank sheet of paper for larger Pict-o-Words).

3. Have students write their assigned vocabulary word and its definition in their own words on one sticky note. On the other sticky note, ask students to copy the text that includes the vocabulary word.

4. Have students create a visual that synthesizes the vocabulary word and the meaning of the word on the notecard or blank sheet of paper.

5. Allow students to present their Pict-o-Words to the class. If need be, ask them to provide an explanation of the way the visual connects to the meaning of the word.

6. Add Pict-o-Words to the Word Wall.

examples

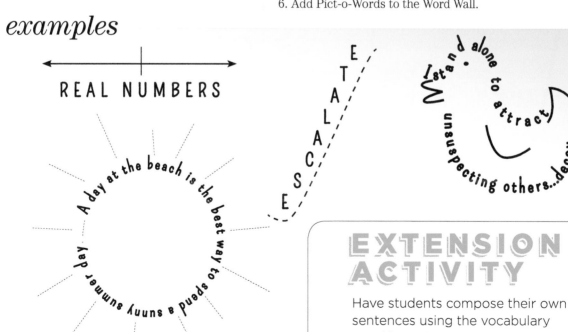

EXTENSION ACTIVITY

Have students compose their own sentences using the vocabulary word in context.

39 Yes/No, Guess the Word

What it's all about

This activity can be completed at the beginning or end of a class period. Not only does it help students build independent strategies to learn new vocabulary, but it motivates students to make new vocabulary part of their everyday language.

Directions

1. Write vocabulary words from a recent unit of study on sticky notes, one word per note. Be sure to have one sticky note for every student in class.

2. Place a sticky note on the back of every student as they walk into class.

3. Have students mingle and ask yes/no questions to try to find out which word they are. Students who discover their "identities" can remove the sticky note, but they should still mingle and help others try to discover their words.

examples

Stereotype

Archetype

EXTENSION ACTIVITIES

Have students use their "sticky note word" in a Targeted Ticket Out. (See page 55 for instructions.)

40 Password

What it's all about

Password is a game of clues. As students provide synonyms, antonyms, and descriptions for a target vocabulary word, they are given multiple opportunities to practice with words. This game can be played on all levels and in all content areas.

Password can be played over a period of weeks, thereby keeping the vocabulary words in constant focus for students.

Directions

1. Prepare a list of five words and place them in an envelope.

2. Divide the class into two teams, A and B.

3. Choose one team to go first in the opening round, and randomly choose one student to represent the team.

4. Give the representative student an envelope and two minutes to provide clues for the words on the list. *(Note: If the student is having difficulty thinking of clues, offer him/her the freedom to skip the word and go on to the next.)*

5. Award one point to the team when a word is identified correctly.

6. Choose a representative for the other team, and give them an envelope of words to describe to their teammates.

7. Do this activity on a daily basis.

8. Continue the game over a period of weeks so that every student has a chance to provide clues.

9. Acknowledge and/or reward the winning team.

EXTENSION ACTIVITY

Have students play Password in pairs.

41 Few Clues

What it's all about

In this guessing game, students use verbal cues to describe a target vocabulary word, but they do not use common "off limits" (decided ahead of time by the teacher) words or phrases typically associated with the definition decided upon in class.

As students play this game, they must use their own words to describe the vocabulary word, not the words provided in the class definition. With this strategy, students think critically and reach a deeper understanding of vocabulary words.

Directions

1. Randomly assign a vocabulary word to each student.

2. Have students write the target vocabulary word in all capital letters at the top of a notecard and then circle the word. Below the word, have students write a list of 4 "forbidden" words that may not be spoken as clues.

3. Collect the cards and shuffle them.

4. Divide the class into two teams, and have each team select a person to read the clues. As each team takes its turn, the reader reminds the team not to use any of the "forbidden" words.

5. As the game proceeds, the team has one minute to guess the word. If the team guesses the word, they earn a point, and the next team gets a turn. If the team does not guess the word, the opposing team gets an opportunity to steal the point. The teams continue to take turns until all the cards have been used. The team with the most points is the winning team.

examples

NOBLE GAS

Forbidden Words: helium, element, inert, odorless

ABSOLUTE VALUE

Forbidden Words: zero, positive, negative, real number

EXTENSION ACTIVITIES

Play a version of Few Clues. In this version, the artist may only sketch/draw previously "forbidden" words as clues, and their teammates attempt to guess the vocabulary word.

Have students select a vocabulary word, think of three words that are often used to describe that word, and those will be the forbidden words.

42 Visual Clues

What it's all about

Clues in this game are given through visuals. Marzano (2004) explains that the use of non-linguistically based strategies can produce a gain of 34% in vocabulary learning. This quick, fun activity provides the multiple exposures and deep understanding needed to promote vocabulary learning.

Directions

1. Select approximately 8-12 vocabulary words to be used in the game, and write them on notecards or small slips of paper.

2. Place the words in a brown bag or envelope so students may choose a word.

3. Divide students into two teams. Depending on the number of students and the number of vocabulary words you use, the class may be divided into four teams with two games taking place concurrently.

4. Have each team choose an artist, and have the artist select a vocabulary word from the bag or envelope.

5. Set the timer for one minute. Without speaking or gesturing, the artist must draw clues that help his/her teammates identify the vocabulary word. If the team guesses the correct vocabulary word, they earn a point. If they do not guess the word within one minute, the opposing team has a chance to steal the point.

6. The teams continue taking turns until all of the words have been selected.

EXTENSION ACTIVITY

Rather than drawing clues, exclusively, to elicit the correct response from their teammates, give students the opportunity to use other techniques to work with words. For example, using a dice, assign a number to a technique to describe words. Allow the clue "giver" to roll the dice to determine which method he/she will use to convey the meaning of the target word. The methods could include asking students who roll a 1 or 2 to draw a visual clue; asking students who roll a 3 or 4 to act out the word, like they would in charades; or asking students who roll a 5 or 6 to create a clay model (or other art medium) to describe the vocabulary word.

43 Word Wall Detectives

What it's all about
To make a Word Wall effective and usable, challenge students to categorize the words on the Word Wall in a closed sort.

Directions

1. Place students in groups of three.

2. Give students a list of categories such as:
   - Science: living/non-living; animal mothers/animal babies; liquid/solid; animal/reptile
   - Math: number/color; shape/size; input/output
   - Social Studies: city/country; culture/religion; boundary/religion
   - English Language Arts: adverbs/adjectives; nouns/verbs; contractions/other; present tense/past tense

   (Note: If the vocabulary words on the Word Wall lend themselves to other categories, feel free to adjust these examples to fit your needs.)

3. Have students look at the Word Wall in the classroom and group words in the categories assigned.

4. Choose one person from each group to give examples from one category. Write the lists on the board for all to see.

5. Rotate to different groups to address all categories students worked on in class.

6. Ask students to judge the completed lists and determine their accuracy. If they believe there are errors in the way the words are sorted, ask students how the words should be adjusted and why.

EXTENSION ACTIVITY

Have students design a list of original categories and work with partners to assign words from a past, present, or future unit of study to the new categories.

44 SWAT

What it's all about

SWAT is a vocabulary game that actually uses fly swatters to swat at a word on the Word Wall or board.

This activity requires students to listen to the definition of a vocabulary word read aloud by the teacher and to locate it quickly. As students engage in this activity, they develop auditory skills, and they reinforce their knowledge of vocabulary words.

Directions

1. Group students into two teams and have each team form a single-file line.

2. Give the first student in each team/line a fly swatter, and ask this student to stand. *(Note: For safety reasons, instruct students to hold fly swatters on the shoulder while the definition/clue is read aloud.)*

3. Tell students they will hear the definition/clue of the selected vocabulary word twice before they are allowed to swat. *(Note: This provides wait time for students.)*

4. Have students respond to the definition/clue by "swatting" the correct vocabulary word on the Word Wall or board. The first student to swat the correct answer gets a point for the team.

5. Have students then hand off the fly swatter to the next person in the line, and ask them to move to the back of the line.

VOCABULARY GAMES

example POLYGON

EXTENSION ACTIVITY

In an advanced version of SWAT, have students use the vocabulary word in a sentence before they swat the term.

List of Latin and Greek Morphemes

Prefixes

a, ab	away, from, apart, away from	avert, astringent, abnormal, abstain, ablation, abduct, abscission
a, an	not, without	asymmetrical, amoral, anachronism
ad	to, toward	adhesion, adjoin
ambi, amphi	both	amphitheater, ambiguous, ambivalent
ante	before	antecedent, anterior, anteroom
anti	against	antiaircraft, antipathy, anticlimax
bene	good	benevolence, beneficent, benefit, benevolent
circum	around, round, surrounding	circumstance, circumference, circumscribe, circumnavigate
con, com, co	together, with	continue, communal, connection, cooperation, company
contra, counter	against, opposed to	contraindicate, contradiction, countermeasure, counterplot, counterpoint
de	down from, away from, reverse	departure, derailment, demerit, debrief
dia	through	dialectic, dialogue, diagnosis, diameter, diagonal
dis	opposite of, away	disinherit, disperse, disenfranchise, dismissal
dys	ill, bad, impaired, difficult	dysplasia, dysfunctional, dyslexia
epi	upon, above	epidemic, epigram, epitaph, epicenter, epidermis, epilogue
ex	out, out of, away from, formerly	exoskeleton, exotic, exterior, exit, exclusion
fore	in front	forehead, forecast, foreshadow, foreclose, forebode, forearm

hyper	over, above, beyond, excessively	hyperactive, hypersensitive, hypersonic, hyperventilate
hypo	under, beneath, below	hypochondriac, hypothermia, hypodermic, hypodermal
il	not	illiterate, illegal, illogical, illusion
in	in, into, within	incision, insertion, inclusion
in-	not	incredible, inhospitable, infinite, infinitesimal, incapable
inter-	between, among	interact, interpret, intervene, intercept, interstate
intra, intro	within	intramurals, intravenous, introduction, introspection
luc	light	lucent, lucid, translucent
mega-	large, great	megawatt, megahertz, megaphone, megabyte
mis	wrong(ly), incorrect(ly)	misunderstood, mistake, misspell, misprint, miscalculate
multi-	many	multisyllabic, multicolored, multiply, multitude, multivitamin
neo-	new	neophyte, Neolithic, neonatal, neoplasm
non-	not	nonentity, nonpayment, nonprofessional, noninvasive, nonsense
nov-	new	novel, novelist, novelty, novice
omni-	all	omnipresent, omnipotent, omniscient
pan-	all	pandemic, panacea, panorama, pantheism, panic
per-	through, throughout, over, large, high	perceive, perfuse, pervade, pervasive, perfect
peri	around	peritoneum, periscope, perimeter
poly-	many	polygon, polygamy, polyester, polyethylene, polyglot, polytechnic, polysyllabic

Prefixes

post-	after	postpone, postscript, postoperative, postnasal, postpartum, post-war
pre-	before	preview, premier, premium, preface, prewar
prim-	first	primer, prime, primary, primitive
pro-	in favor of, forward, in place of	probiotics, project, projectile, pronoun
proto-	first	protoplasm, prototype, protocol, proton
re-	back, again	repetitive, retraction, revert, repetition, retrace, refurbish, regenerate
retro-	back, backward	retrospect, retroactive, retrograde, retrorocket
se-	away, apart	segregation, seclusion, secession, sequester
sub-	under, below	subterfuge, submarine, subterranean
super	over, above, beyond	superfluous, supervisory
sym-, syn-	together, with	symbiotic, symphony, symmetry, symbol, symptom, synthesis, synchronize, synonym, synonymous
trans-	across, over	transport, transcend, transition, translate, transmission
ultra	excessively	ultramodern, ultrasound, ultralight, ultraviolet

acer-, acr-	sharp, bitter	acerbic, acid, acrid, acerbate
alter-	other	alter ego, alternative, alternate
ambul-	walk	ambulatory, ambulance, amble, somnambular
amor	love	amiable, enamored, amorous
annu, enni	ear	annual, annually, anniversary, biennial, centennial, perennial
anthropo-	man	misanthrope, philanthropy, anthropology
aqua	water	aqueduct, aqueous, aquarium
arch	ruler, chief, first	archdiocese, archenemy, monarch, anarchy
aster	star	astronomy, asterisk, astronaut
aud, audit	hear, listen to	audiology, auditorium, audition, audience
bene	good	benefactor, benevolent, benign, benediction
bibl-	book	bibliography, bibliophile, Bible
bio-	life	biome, biometrics, biology, biography, biopic
calor-	heat	caloric, calorie
cap-	take, hold	capable, capture
capit, capt	head, chief, leader	captain, caption, capital, captor
cardi-	heart	cardiovascular, cardiogram, cardiology, cardiac
carn-	flesh	carnal, carnivorous, incarnate, reincarnation
caus, caut	burn	caustic, cauldron, cauterize, holocaust
cause, cuse ,cus	cause, motive	excuse, accusation, because, cause

Roots

cede, cess	move, yield	procedure, concede, recede, precede, accede, success
chrom-	color	chromosome, polychrome, chromatic
chron-	time	chronology, synchronize, chronicle, chronological
clud	shut	conclude, include, exclude
corp, corpor	body	corporation, corpse, corporal
crat, cracy	power, rule	democrat, aristocrat, democracy, theocracy
cred-	believe	credit, credible, incredible, credo
crux, cruc	cross	crucify, crucifix, crucial, crucible, crux
crypt	secret, hidden	crypt, cryptic, cryptogram
culpa	blame	culprit, culpable
cur, curs	run, course	concurrent, current, incur, occur, precursor, cursive, cursor
dem-	people	epidemic, democracy, demography
derm-	skin	hypodermic, dermatology, epidermis, taxidermy
deus	god	deity, deify
dic(t)	tell, speak	dictum, dictionary, dictation, dictate, dictator, edict, contradict, benediction
dorm-	sleep	dormitory, dormancy, dormant
dox	belief	doxology, paradox, orthodox
duc(t)	lead	seduce, produce, reduce, induce, introduce, conduct
dyna-	power	dynamite, hydrodynamics, dynamic, dynasty
equ-	equal	equitable, equinox, equilibrium, equivalent

Roots

fac-	make, do	manufacture, fact, factory
fer	bear, carry	fertile, ferry, transfer, refer, infer, defer, aquifer
fid	faith, trust	fidelity, confederate, confidence, infidelity, infidel, federal
flu, flux	flowing	influenza, influence, fluid, flush, confluence, fluently, fluctuate
fort-	strong	fortress, fortitude, fort, fortify
fract-	break	refract, infraction, fracture
frater	brother	fraternity, fraternal, fraternize
gen-	race, birth, kind	generate, genetic, eugenics, genesis, genealogy, generation, antigen
geo-	earth	geometry, geography, geocentric, geology, geothermal
greg-	flock, herd	congregation, congregate, gregarious
gress	go	progress, progression, egress
gyn-	woman	gynecology, gynecologist
hetero	different	heterogeneous, heteromorphic, heteronym
homo, homeo	same	homogenize, homogeneous, homonym, homeostasis
homo-	man	homage, Homo sapiens
hydr-	water	hydrate, dehydrate, hydrant, hydraulic, hydrogen, hydrophobia
jac, jec	throw	projectile, projector, eject
lact-	milk	lactose, lactate
junct-	join	juncture, junction, adjunct, conjunction
lat-	side	lateral, equilateral, unilateral
laud	praise	applause, laudable, plausible, applaud
lect-	gather, choose, read	collection, lecture, election, electorate
leg, legis	law	legislate, legal, legislature, legitimize
lith	stone	monolithic, megalith, batholith, Neolithic

Roots

locu, loqu	speak	eloquent, loquacious, colloquial, circumlocution, elocution
log, logy	speech, word, study of	catalogue, dialogue, prologue, psychology, logical, zoology
magn(i)	large, great	magnificent, manufacture, magnate, magnitude, magnum
mal	bad, evil	malnourished, malignant, malicious, malfunction, malcontent,
man, manu	hand	manual, manicure, manacle, maneuver, emancipate, manufacture
meter, metr	measure	meter, barometer, thermometer, symmetry
micro	small	microscope, microwave, micrometer, microbe
mit, miss	send	emit, remit, commit, submit, permit, transmit, mission, permission, missile
mob, mov, mot	move	motor, movie, motivate, emotional, mobile, movie, motivation, emote, immortal
mute	change	mutate, mutation, immutable
nasc, nat	birth, spring forth	nascent, innate, natal, native, renaissance, nativity
nihil, nil	nothing	annihilate
noct-	night	nocturnal
nym	name	antonym, synonym, acronym, pseudonym, homonym, anonymous
oner, onus	burden	onerous, onus
ortho	straight, right, correct	orthopedic, orthodontist, unorthodox, orthodox
pac-	peace	Pacific Ocean, pacify, pacifier, pacifist
path-	feeling, disease	telepathy, sympathy, antipathy, apathy, pathos
pecc-	fault, sin	impeccable, peccadilloes

ped, pod	foot	pedal, pedestrian, impede, centipede, tripod, podiatry, podium
pel, puls	urge, drive	compel, impel, expel, repel, propel, pulse, impulse, pulsate, compulsory, repulsive
pend, pen	hang	pendulum, pendant, suspend, appendage, pensive, impending
phil-	love	philanthropist, philosophy
phob-	fear	claustrophobia, agoraphobia, homophobia, arachnophobia
phon-	sound	phonograph, telephone, homophone, euphonious, phonetic
photo-	light	photographic, photogenic, photosynthesis
physio-	nature	physiological, physiology
plac	please, appease	placebo, placid, placate, complacent
plen, plete	fill	complete, replenish, plentiful, deplete
pli, plic, plex	fold, bend	complicate, pliable, multiplication
polis	city	metropolis, police, megalopolis, politics, acropolis, Indianapolis
pon, pos	place, put	component, postpone, component, position, deposit, proponent
popul-	people	population, populous, popular
port-	carry	transport, import, export, support, report, portfolio
preci-	price	precious, depreciate, appreciate
prim-	first, early	primal, primary, primitive, primeval
pseudo-	false	pseudonym, pseudoscience
psych-	mind	psychiatry, psyche, psychology, psychosis
pulmo-	lung	pulmonary
pung-, punct	point	pungent, punctual, puncture
quasi-	like, but not really	quasi-scientific, quasi-official, quasi-war, quasi-corporation

Roots

sanct-	holy	sanctuary, sanctimonious, sanction
scien-	know, knowledge	science, conscience, omniscient
scope	sight	microscope, telescope, kaleidoscope, periscope, stethoscope
scrib, script	write	scribe, scribble, inscribe, describe, subscribe, script, manuscript
sequ, secut	follow	consequence, sequence, sequel, consecutive
sol-	alone	solstice, solo, solitary, solitude, solitaire
solv, solut	loosen	solvent, solve, solution, absolve, resolution, resolute, resolve
somn-	sleep	somnambulant, somnolent, somniferous
son-	sound	resonance, resonate, sonic, unison
soph-	wise	sophomore, philosopher, sophisticated
spec(t)	look	spectator, spectacle, aspect, inspect, speculate, respect, prospect, retrospective, expect
spir-	breath, breathe	respirator, aspire, expire, perspire, conspire
string, strict	tighten	stringent, astringent, stricture, strict, restriction, constrict
stru, struct-	build	construct, instruct, destruction, structure
tang, tact, tig	touch	tangible, intangible, tactile, contact, contiguous
tele-	far, far-off	teleport, television, telephone, telegram, telescope, telephoto, telecast, telepathy
tend, tens	hold	contend, pretend, intend, superintendent, tendency, tension
terra-	earth	terrarium, territory, terrain, terrestrial, extraterrestrial, terra firma
theo-	god	theology, atheism, polytheism, monotheism
tom-	cut	anatomy, atom, appendectomy, dichotomy, tonsillectomy, dichotomy
tort-	twist	distortion, torture, retort, distort, contort, torturous
tract-	draw, drag	retractable, attract, tractor, subtract, abstract, extract

Roots

ven(t)	come	ventricle, ventilate, vent, convention, venue, avenue, venture, event, advent, prevent
vert, vers	turn	convertible, controversial, avert, divert, invert, versatile, reversible
vid, vis	see	evidence, providence, video, provide, visual, vista, visit, vision
viv	live	survivor, vivacious, revive, vivid,
voc- *(voz, voice)*	call, speak, voice	vocabulary, convocation, vocal, vocation, avocation

Latin and Greek Numbers

One	uni	union, unilateral, uniform, university, united
	mono	monotheism, monastic, monotone, monologue
Two	du(o)	duplication, duet, duplex,
	bi	biweekly, bilingual, bicycle, binomial
Three	tri	tricycle, triad, triangle, triceps, trichromatic, triplicate
Four	quad(ri) (ra)	quadruplets, quadruple, quadrangle, quadriceps, quadruped
	tetra	tetragonal, tetrahedron, tetrameter, tetrapod
Five	quin	quintuplet, quintet, quintessence
	pent(a)	pentameter, pentagon, Pentateuch, pentathlon, pentacle, Pentecost
Six	sex	sextant, sexagenarian, sextuplet, sextet
	hex(a)	hexagram, hexadecimal, hexachord, hexagon, hexameter
Seven	sept	septennial, septet, septuagenarian
	hept(a)	heptahedron, heptameter, heptagon
Eight	octo	octagon, octogenarian, octave, octet, octopus
Nine	non	nonagenarian, nonagon
Ten	dec	decagon, decahedron, decade, decalogue, decameter, decimal
One hundred	cent	centipede, centimeter, centennial, century
One thousand	mil-, milli-	milliliter, millimeter, millennium, millipede, milliliter, millisecond

These books can be used to encourage word appreciation and vocabulary acquisition.

Since the goal is to give students multiple exposures to new words, reading books to introduce new vocabulary gives students an immediate advantage. Instantly, it places the words – and strategies for learning them – in context!

While some of the following books are children's books, students in the secondary grades love to listen to them too. Chosen correctly, they can be used to introduce or complement a unit of vocabulary.

Alphabet Soup by Kate Banks. (Dragonfly Books, 1988) This charming picture book tells the story of a young boy who spells words in his soup. His words cause the animals, people, and objects he spells to appear.

Word Wizard by Cathryn Falwell. (Houghton Mifflin, 1998) This book tells the story of a young girl who rearranges letters in her alphabet cereal, making one word change to another — like ocean to canoe.

The Phantom Tollbooth by Norton Juster. (Random House, 1964) In this book, the main character discovers that words and phrases are more than just marks on a page. Here, Milo meets King Azaz the Unabridged and his advisers, the Duke of Definition, the Minister of Meaning, the Earl of Essence, the Count of Connotation, and the Undersecretary of Understanding. But this is only the beginning, there's Dictionopolis, a place to feast on synonyms before traveling to the Lands Beyond.

The Westing Game by Ellen Raskin. (Puffin, 1992) This mystery compels readers to look closely at words as clues in a race to help them discover who Samuel Westing really is and who will inherit his fortune.

A Very Witchy Spelling Bee by George Shannon & Mark Fearing. (Houghton Mifflin, 2013) Words like c-a-t can be changed to c-o-a-t with a twist of letters and the addition of one more letter. In this story, a couple of feuding witches compete to win a Halloween spelling bee. Cordelia and Beulah Divine eventually change f-i-e-n-d into f-r-i-e-n-d and learn to appreciate each other's skills.

The Grapes of Math by Greg Tang. (Scholastic, 2001) This book challenges children to solve problems in new and unexpected ways. Good for parents and teachers too!

These books can be used to focus on word histories.

A Chartreuse Leotard in a Magenta Limousine and Other Words Named after People and Places by Lynda Graham-Barber. (Hyperion, Newberry, 1995)

Dictionary of Word Origins: A History of the Words, Expressions, and Clichés We Use by Jordan Almond. (Carol, 1995)

Guppies in Tuxedos and Other Funny Eponyms by Marvin Terban. (Clarion, 1988)

Where in the Word?: Extraordinary Stories Behind 801 Ordinary Words by David Mushcell. (Prima, 1990)

These books can be used to focus on the humor of multiple meaning words, idioms, and homonyms.

Amelia Bedelia books by Peggy Parish. (Scholastic)

The King Who Rained, A Little Pigeon Toad, and A Chocolate Moose for Dinner by Fred Gwynne. (Simon & Schuster)

Alexander, P.A. (1984). Training analogical reasoning skills in the gifted. *Roeper Review, 6*(4), 191-193.

Anderson, R.C., & Nagy, W.E. (1992). The vocabulary conundrum. *American Educator, 16*(4), 14-18, 44-47.

Beck, I.L., McKeown, M.G., & Kucan, L. (2002). *Bringing words to life: Robust vocabulary instruction.* New York: Guilford Press.

Blachowicz, C., & Fisher, P (2005). *Teaching vocabulary in all classrooms* (2nd ed.). Columbus, OH: Merrill/Prentice-Hall.

Buehl, D. (2008). *Classroom strategies for interactive reading.* Newark, DE: International Reading Association.

Cattell, R.B. (1987). *Intelligence: Its structure, growth and action* (Rev. ed.). Amsterdam: North Holland Press.

Dutro, S., & Moran, C. (2003). Rethinking English language instruction: An architectural approach. In G. Garcia (Ed.), *English learners: Reaching the highest level of English literacy* (pp. 227-258). Newark, DE: International Reading Association.

Frayer, D., Frederick, W.C., & Klausmeier, H.J. (1969). *Schema for testing the level of concept mastery.* Madison, WI: Wisconsin Research and Development Center for Cognitive Learning, University of Wisconsin.

Graves, M.F. (2006). *The vocabulary book: Learning & instruction.* New York: Teachers College Press.

Hall, S. (1990). *Using picture storybooks to teach literary devices: Recommended books for children and young adults.* Phoenix, AZ: Oryx Press.

Kagan, S. (1990). Cooperative learning for students limited in language proficiency. In M. Brubacher, R. Payne, & K. Rickett (Eds.), *Perspectives on small group learning: Theory and practice* (pp. 202-223). Oakville, Ontario, Canada: Rubicon Publishing, Inc.

Marzano, R. (2004). *Building academic background knowledge for academic achievement: Research on what works in schools.* Alexandria, VA: Association for Supervision and Curriculum Development.

Marzano, R., & Pickering D. (2005). *Building academic vocabulary: Teacher's manual.* Alexandria, VA: Association for Supervision and Curriculum Development.

Marzano, R., Pickering, D., & Pollack, J. (2001). *Research-based strategies for increasing student achievement: Classroom instruction that works.* Alexandria, VA: Association for Supervision and Curriculum Development.

National Institute for Literacy. (2006). *What content-area teachers should know about adolescent literature.* Jessup, MD: National Institute of Child Health and Human Development. Retrieved at http://lincs.ed.gov/publications/pdf/ adolescent_literacy07.pdf

National Institute of Child Health and Human Development (NICHD). (2000). Report of the National Reading Panel. *Teaching children to read: An evidence-based assessment of the scientific research literature on reading and its implications for reading instruction (NIH Publication No. 00-4769).* Washington, DC: U.S. Government Printing Office. Retrieved at http://www.nichd.nih.gov/ publications/pubs/ nrp/pages/smallbook.aspx

Novak, J.D., Moon, B.M., Hoffman, R.R., & Canas, A.J. (2011). *Applied concept mapping: Capturing, analyzing, and organizing information.* Boca Raton, FL: CRC Press.

O'Neal, D., & Ringler, M. (2010). Broadening our view of linguistic diversity. *Phi Delta Kappa,* 91(7), 48-52.

RAND Reading Study Group. (2002). *Reading for understanding: Toward an R&D program in reading comprehension.* Santa Monica, CA: RAND. Retrieved at http:// www.gpo.gov/fdsys/pkg/ERIC-ED463559/pdf/ERIC-ED463559.pdf

Ratterman, M.J., & Gentner, D. (1998). More evidence for a relational shift in the development of analogy: Children's performance on a causal-mapping task. *Cognitive Development,* 13(4), 453-478.

Smith, F. (1990). *To think.* New York: Teachers College Press.

Stahl, S.A., & Fairbanks, M. (1986). The effects of vocabulary instruction: A model-based meta-analysis. *Review of Educational Research. 56*(1), 82-110.

Zwiers, J. (2008). *Essential practices for content classrooms.* San Francisco, CA: John Wiley & Sons.

PHOTOGRAPHY CREDITS

Classroom photos on pages 19, 37, 43, 46, 49, 52, 61, 67, and 76 appear courtesy of the Fredericksburg Independent School District.

Classroom photos on pages 9, 12, 15, 23, and 36 appear courtesy of the Irving Independent School District.

Classroom photo (at right) on page 36 appears courtesy of the Lake Worth Independent School District.

SEIDLITZ PRODUCT ORDER FORM

Three ways to order

- **FAX** completed order form with payment information to **(949) 481-3864**
- **PHONE** order information to **(210) 315-7119**
- **ORDER ONLINE** at **www.seidlitzeducation.com**

Pricing, specifications, and availability subject to change without notice.

PRODUCT	PRICE	QUANTITY	TOTAL
NEW! Talk Read Talk Write: A Practical Approach to Learning in the Secondary Classroom	**$29.95**		
NEW! ELLs in Texas: What Administrators Need to Know	**$29.95**		
NEW! Vocabulary Now! 44 Strategies All Teachers Can Use	**$29.95**		
Diverse Learner Flip Book	**$26.95**		
ELPS Flip Book	**$19.95**		
Academic Language Cards and Activity Booklet, ENGLISH	**$19.95**		
Academic Language Cards, SPANISH	**$9.95**		
Sheltered Instruction Plus	**$19.95**		
RTI for ELLs Fold-Out	**$16.95**		
7 Steps to a Language-Rich Interactive Classroom	**$29.95**		
7 Pasos para crear un aula interactiva y rica en lenguaje SPANISH	**$29.95**		
Language & Literacy for ELLs Workbook	**$29.95**		
Language & Literacy for ELLs Handbbook	**$29.95**		
38 Great Academic Language Builders	**$24.95**		
An Exemplary Disciplinary Alternative Education Program (DAEP) Handbook with CD-ROM	**$29.95**		
Navigating the ELPS: Using the Standards to Improve Instruction for English Learners	**$24.95**		
Navigating the ELPS: Math	**$29.95**		
Navigating the ELPS: Science	**$29.95**		
Navigating the ELPS: Social Studies	**$29.95**		
Navigating the ELPS: Language Arts and Reading	**$34.95**		
'Instead Of I Don't Know' Poster, Elementary ENGLISH ☐ Elementary ☐ Secondary	**$9.95**		
'Instead Of I Don't Know' Poster, Elementary SPANISH (Elementary only)	**$9.95**		
'Please Speak In Complete Sentences' Poster ENGLISH	**$9.95**		
'Please Speak In Complete Sentences' Poster SPANISH	**$9.95**		

SHIPPING $14.95 for 1-15 items, plus $1.05 each per additional items over 15.
5-7 business days to ship. If needed sooner please call for rates.
TAX EXEMPT? please fax a copy of your certificate along with order.

DISCOUNT	
SHIPPING	
TAX	
TOTAL	

NAME

SHIPPING ADDRESS   CITY   STATE, ZIP

PHONE NUMBER   EMAIL ADDRESS

TO ORDER BY FAX
to **(949)481-3864**
please complete
credit card info *or*
attach purchase order

☐ **Visa**   ☐ **MasterCard**   ☐ **Discover**   ☐ **AMEX**

CC#   Exp. Date:

Signature

☐ **Purchase Order attached**
please make P.O. out to **Seidlitz Education**

For information about Seidlitz Education products
and professional development, please contact us at

(210) 315-7119 | kathy@johnseidlitz.com
56 Via Regalo, San Clemente, CA 92673
www.seidlitzeducation.com

Giving kids the gift of **academic language.**™

REVO33114